Keep It R.E.A.L!

Keep It R.E.A.L!

Relevant, Engaging, and Affirming Literacy for Adolescent English Learners

Mary Amanda Stewart

TEACHERS COLLEGE PRESS
TEACHERS COLLEGE | COLUMBIA UNIVERSITY
NEW YORK AND LONDON

NATIONAL WRITING PROJECT

Published simultaneously by Teachers College Press, 1234 Amsterdam Avenue, New York, NY 10027 and National Writing Project, 2105 Bancroft Way, Berkeley, CA 94720-1042

Through its mission, the National Writing Project (NWP) focuses the knowledge, expertise, and leadership of our nation's educators on sustained efforts to help youth become successful writers and learners. NWP works in partnership with local writing project sites, located on nearly 200 university and college campuses, to provide high-quality professional development in schools, universities, libraries, museums, and after-school programs. NWP envisions a future where every person is an accomplished writer, engaged learner, and active participant in a digital, interconnected world.

Cover images: Polaroid frame by Felipe y Natalia Millán Assler / Flickr; Young man reading by Marc Romanelli / Getty Images.

Figure 3.1 printed courtesy of the United States Holocaust Memorial Museum

Library of Congress Cataloging-in-Publication Data is available at loc.gov

Names: Stewart, Mary Amanda, 1979- author.
Title: Keep it R.E.A.L.! : relevant, engaging, and affirming literacy for adolescent English learners / Mary Amanda Stewart.
Other titles: Keep it real!
Description: New York, NY : Teachers College Press, 2017. | Includes bibliographical references and index.
Identifiers: LCCN 2017031700| ISBN 9780807758700 (pbk. : alk. paper) | ISBN 9780807776650 (ebook)
Subjects: LCSH: English language--Study and teaching (Secondary)--United States--Foreign speakers. | English language--Study and teaching (Middle school)--United States--Foreign speakers. | Second language acquisition--Methodology. | Education, Bilingual--United States.
Classification: LCC PE1128.A2 S835 2017 | DDC 428.0071/273--dc23
LC record available at https://lccn.loc.gov/2017031700

ISBN 978-0-8077-5870-0 (paper)
ISBN 978-0-8077-7665-0 (ebook)

Printed on acid-free paper
Manufactured in the United States of America

24 23 22 21 20 19 18 17   8 7 6 5 4 3 2 1

For Sparky, who loves reading and passed it down to my mother who passed it down to me.

Contents

A Note to the Reader

This book is about putting research-based ideas and activities into practice. To assist in understanding terminology from various fields, vocabulary related to adolescent literacy, second language acquisition, and bilingualism are introduced the first time in bold and then included in the Glossary at the end of the book for your reference. Then, to help you try out new instructional ideas in your classroom, each chapter concludes with an Action Time box that suggests very specific actions you can take to initiate R.E.A.L. instruction. There are also specific book recommendations, websites, and other resources mentioned throughout—within the text, tables and figures, appendices, and a Literature Cited section at the end of the book. Most of these resources were used with adolescent English learners at varying levels of English acquisition from 2013 to 2016; however, I have also included more recent titles that I think would support R.E.A.L. instruction. Additionally, because new texts are disseminated daily, I have included many online sites where you can locate more recent resources. The literature specifically mentioned in this book is merely a launching place for exciting R.E.A.L. instruction to occur.

I think you will get the most out of this book if you put some of the activities suggested into practice as you read. For preservice teachers who do not have access to a classroom, this can be accomplished by reading some of the suggested literature to use in your future classrooms with English learners after you complete each chapter. If possible, observe actual secondary classrooms with English learners as you read and use that experience to guide your understanding of this book. If you are currently in a classroom environment with English learners where you work as a teacher, instructional specialist, literacy coach, or student-teacher, I recommend that you attempt at least one new activity suggested in each chapter before moving on. Then, continue the same pattern throughout the chapters, taking risks to try out new reading or reader response activities with your English learners. Most important, have fun reading and responding in your literacy learning community!

CHAPTER 1

Keep It R.E.A.L. for Adolescent English Learners

Valeria[1] is an 11th-grade student who came from El Salvador 2 years ago with only her younger sister and "coyotes" (human smugglers). Paying an exorbitant amount of money to the coyotes, she escaped El Salvador and treacherously passed through two other countries in hiding to arrive at the U.S. border where she was captured by immigration officials and sent to a detention center to await her fate. Why would a teenage girl embark on such a dangerous journey? To simplify a complex reason that draws many young people like Valeria: It is because she wants to be in your classroom. She took great risks and left her mother behind, all for a better life. To her, that better life of opportunities starts with learning English, graduating from high school, pursuing postsecondary education, and possessing the literacy and language skills needed to become a detective in her new country. She would indeed make an incredible bilingual detective, but in order to get there, she needs the best education we can possibly provide her. She not only needs the literacy abilities to perform well in school, but also to have agency within an ever-changing immigration system that affects her status in the United States and her ability to reunite with her mother. The literacy learning we afford or deny Valeria will directly affect her social mobility.

It is Valeria, more than any other student I've taught, who reminds me, even challenges me, to "keep it real." The Online Slang Dictionary (Rader, 2017) defines *keep it real* in the following ways: "to stay true to one's self; to resist the temptation to be fake; to be true to 'the game,' whatever the game happens to be."

My game is teaching—specifically, teaching literacy to adolescent **English learners (ELs)**, students in the dynamic process of **second language acquisition**. Like many of you, one of the reasons I became a teacher was because I love to read and share literature with others. I additionally chose to focus on English learners because I'm fascinated by other languages and cultures. My passions come together when I teach language and literacy to students from around the world through writing bilingual poetry, reading together, and

---

1. All names of students and teachers used in this book, besides my own, are pseudonyms. Additionally, the names of people in student writing have been given pseudonyms.

learning from students as they share their unique lived experiences with me. Keep it R.E.A.L. (relevant, engaging, and affirming literacy) is my manifesto about who I am as an educator and what it is I do—for Valeria, and for all adolescents acquiring English as an additional language. This is my game.

Yet I am aware of the many challenges that confront secondary teachers of English learners regarding language and literacy instruction—their game. Although I acknowledge those challenges (standardized testing, curricular uniformity, unrealistic time frames), they do not have to define our teaching. We can, indeed, resist the temptation to be fake, to merely teach to standardized tests with narrow views of literacy, and stay true to our game. R.E.A.L. instruction seeks to find ways over, under, and through any challenge to meet the literacy needs of ELs in the most effective way possible. Even more, R.E.A.L. instruction should be a joyous celebration of learning *from* and *with* your students as you walk with them on their academic journey. It should excite both student and teacher to enter a relevant, engaging, and affirming literacy learning environment—your classroom.

WHAT IS R.E.A.L. INSTRUCTION?

I began using reading and **reader response** as an approach to teaching literacy and language in classrooms with **newcomer** students learning English during a high school summer institute I designed and taught. We read self-selected literature or texts I purposefully chose to connect to particular students and responded before, during, and after our reading in various ways, sharing the connections and meaning we made from the text through discussion, writing, and artistic means. It was exciting, challenging, and rewarding as the students and I were all changed through our community of readers and writers. Former reluctant readers wanted to take books home and students wanted to share their writing with others. Incredible language acquisition occurred as they imparted their culture and experiences with our learning community.

Needing to articulate this approach, I decided on the most important components of this way of teaching, resulting in the acronym R.E.A.L. This form of instruction for adolescent ELs is centered on the students themselves—their unique literacy needs and skills, their individual interests, and their wealth of culturally embedded knowledge. R.E.A.L. instruction begins and ends with the learners entrusted to us and places the focus on them over any other outside influence. Every text and reader response activity mentioned in this book is evaluated under these four criteria:

- Is it *relevant* to students' lives?
- To what degree does it *engage* students' interests within a community?
- How does it *affirm* students' cultural and language identities?
- Does it lend itself to asset-oriented *literacy* instruction?

Relevant to Students' Lives

One of the first teacher education courses I taught at the university level was about adolescent literacy. To ensure that I was up to speed with popular young adult literature, I went to my local library to see what was on their shelves. They had a separate section for teens with some eye-level books on display that were all informational texts about STDs, drugs, and gang violence. Apparently, a librarian had decided these were topics and, consequently, books that would be engaging to teens and would draw them into the young adult section.

Since then, I've questioned the use of the term *relevant*. Who gets to decide what is relevant to whom? As adults, we often determine what is relevant to youth based on poorly informed stereotypes, overgeneralized experiences with one individual, or what we want to be significant to them. Sciurba's (2014) research with adolescent boys of color and how they respond to texts reminds us that relevance is a complex notion. She explains that teachers often make judgments based on students' gender, race, or cultural background in connecting them to literature. Admittedly, I have been one of those teachers, making well-intentioned mistakes in attempting to connect youth to meaningful books and response activities. Sciurba's (2014) suggestions to prevent these overgeneralizations is to interview students—to get to know them and better understand how they might, or might not, relate to a text, unit of study, or instructional activity. Accordingly, we need to learn from our English learners to better understand what is relevant to them.

Therefore, in R.E.A.L. instruction, the relevance of particular texts is determined by the students themselves, giving them a voice in the classroom and requiring that we, as their teachers, know them on a personal level. Ladson-Billings (1995) implores educators to adopt a culturally relevant pedagogy for all students, a plea echoed in the work of Collier (1995), specifically relating to English learners. We must understand elements of both students' **surface culture** and **deep culture**, a topic that will be discussed in Chapter 5. Yet, we cannot assume that what we think is a cultural match or mismatch will always hold true. Ebe (2012) explains the many factors that extend beyond one's race, language, or country of origin that make a piece of literature culturally relevant to a reader. She clarifies that we also need to consider students' age, the time period in which they live, and popular youth culture when determining cultural relevance to a student. Although many of the text selections and reader response activities mentioned in this book directly connect to students' countries of origin or cultures, other topics might also be relevant to them. Adolescent ELs regularly ask me to get them books in English or in their first language (**L1**) that have been turned into popular movies such as the Twilight, Hunger Games, and Divergent series.

Unfortunately, I do not think there is an easy litmus test for relevancy. The relevancy of a particular topic, book, or activity to an individual student might not be determined by a quick yes or no answer. It might require you to live in the gray, somewhere along the relevancy continuum. This uncertainty requires that you provide a broad range of literature and literacy experiences to your students as you learn to be flexible and adapt to their uniqueness. Most important, relevant literacy instruction requires that you value your students and their opinions, using all the literacy tools available to you to get to know your students and their lived experiences. You should continually ask: What books might students read that they could find personally significant? What reader response activities would be meaningful to accompany their reading?

Sometimes we choose potentially meaningful activities, but we have not sufficiently explained to our students why we are analyzing a poem or writing daily in our journals (these ideas are discussed more in Chapters 3 and 4). Because adolescent English learners need to take ownership of what they are learning (Au, 1998), they should know why they are learning it. They need to understand the relevance of their learning beyond the school setting and recognize how it applies to their lives both present and future.

Consequently, we should put each piece of literature and response activity we choose for the classroom on trial. If we are educators committed to relevant instruction for our ELs, we must provide compelling reasons to our students regarding our curricular and instructional decisions. If our answer to a query about our educational choices is "That's the way we've always done it," we might want to reconsider.

Engaging Students' Interests Within a Community

There are many studies that link students' academic achievement to their academic engagement (Guthrie, Wigfield, & You, 2012) and even more particularly, their reading engagement (Ivey & Broaddus, 2007; Ivey & Johnston, 2013). Reading engagement is usually viewed at the individual level, pertaining to one's attention or effort, the emotional responses to a text, and the use of strategies to comprehend (Ivey & Johnston, 2015). To engage students at that individual level, we must know them individually and learn about their lives and their interests. At times, after really getting to know students, I am quite surprised by their hobbies, interests, or experiences. Sometimes it is too easy to assume that a student from Japan will be interested in manga or a student from Latin America will be into soccer. These default assumptions, though not always correct, can still provide a starting place to offer ideas on what students might want to use literacy to learn about in your classroom. Yet adolescent ELs, like other adolescents, will have unique interests that we as teachers can leverage for their instruction.

For example, while working with a young woman from Colombia, I learned that she had much experience and was very interested in competitive roller-skating and was eager to use literacy to learn more about that topic and share her knowledge with others. Other ELs I've taught want to explore topics as diverse as the citizenship process, sports teams, historical events, or famous people from their countries. Andrés, a student who recently came from Mexico, told me he was very interested in Japanese culture and manga videos. Providing him with literature to explore this interest led him to read books at home and talk about them in English with another student.

However, our instruction does not have to remain in students' established areas of interest. By building on what students are already interested in, you can spark new interests through R.E.A.L. instruction. Using literacy to explore various themes, we might ignite curiosity regarding social justice or discrimination that students previously did not even consider. Nathan, a student from the Democratic Republic of Congo (DRC), became interested in understanding more about slavery after his teacher introduced him to racial discrimination in the United States through their shared reading of a novel. As his class explored slavery through literature, he learned that people from his country were brought to the United States against their will—a fact he had not previously considered deeply. Chen from China, who already knew a lot about Ultimate Fighting Championship (UFC), showed interest in learning about boxing, specifically Muhammad Ali. Although these are very diverse topics, both ideas—slavery and boxing—gave Nathan and Chen reasons to read and complete reader response activities. The key is to reflect on what already interests or potentially could interest your students. What would make them want to come to your classroom each day? What might kindle their curiosity? This could be learning about a less controversial topic like boxing or it could be much more serious, such as learning about slavery.

Ivey and Johnston (2015), however, extend engaged reading to mean much more beyond the individual. They explain: "Our argument is that engaged reading is a fully social, fully human experience that is simultaneously and inseparably individual, relational, emotional, and collective" (p. 319). Therefore, the engagement piece of R.E.A.L. instruction will not only consider students' individual interests, but also their engagement with one another. The goal is to nurture a community of engaged learners where each student feels that he or she has a unique and needed role in the community.

Affirming Students' Cultural and Language Identities

Every curricular and instructional decision we make is a political act (Gee, 2015). Whose stories are incorporated in our classrooms? What perspectives are presented? What cultures and languages would someone think we valued if they looked at our bookshelves?

We convey messages to our students by what we include as well as what we neglect in our curriculum and official classroom activities. Valenzuela (1999) asks us to consider a culture- and language-affirming curriculum as well as a teaching style that entails affirming students' cultural knowledge and ways of knowing, including their cultural concepts of education. This affirmation also includes any languages other than English that they use with friends, at home with family, or in their communities. (I discuss the concept of culture more in Chapter 5 and language in Chapter 6.)

Yet, how might we specifically affirm our English learners? To affirm is an abstract concept that we are not always sure how to put into practice. As a result, we should consider very practical ways to begin affirming our students, such as pronouncing their names correctly, even if doing so requires a lot of practice. This singular act can affirm their culture, language, and family heritage. We also affirm students by greeting them in a way that is appropriate for them; thus, I might shake hands, slightly bow, pat on the back, or exchange a high-five with different students in the same class. It is beneficial to continually think about how we can better affirm our students, understanding the practical ways affirmation manifests itself, to ensure that it is not one of those things we think we are doing, yet we've missed the mark entirely.

We can also affirm students by purposefully bringing their cultures and languages into the curriculum (Nieto & Bode, 2012) through **culturally relevant texts** (Freeman, Freeman, Soto, & Ebe, 2016). Reading and reader response activities should send students the message that their knowledge, values, and experiences are acknowledged and deemed valuable for the literacy learning environment. This can happen by creating sanctioned spaces in our classroom for students to express their cultural and linguistic identities through bilingual writing (Stewart & Hansen-Thomas, 2016) that goes beyond merely allowing students to use their languages. It is not "letting" them use an electronic translator or "tolerating" their L1 conversations with another student. On the contrary, sanctioning is encouraging a purposeful and systematic use of students' cultural and linguistic resources for official classroom activities at certain times and in specific spaces.

When we affirm students, we take action to really see them, allowing us to more effectively teach them (Wickstrom, Araujo, Patterson, Hoki, & Roberts, 2011). Seeing our students' cultures and languages tells them that we value who they are and believe they can be successful in our classrooms without losing themselves. They can learn English while proudly displaying and further developing their L1 abilities. They can learn about cultural norms and practices that differ from their own while maintaining and expressing their loyalties within the classroom. Affirming our ELs through literacy instruction means we encourage them to be who they are in our classrooms.

Asset-Oriented *Literacy* Instruction

R.E.A.L. instruction broadly defines **literacy** as any way we send and receive meaning (Gee, 2015), including areas of development that are commonly associated with the English language arts classroom—"reading, writing, listening, speaking, viewing, and visually representing" (International Reading Association & National Council for Teachers of English, 2006, p. 1). Of course, not all literacies carry the same weight in our society (Harste, 2003), but our classrooms can be a place where all forms of literacy are valued. Funds of knowledge (González, Moll, & Amanti, 2005) represent an idea that takes an **asset-oriented stance** toward instruction—that is, this stance chooses to see students' strengths and purposefully leverages the literacies and ways of knowing, being, doing, and communicating that already exist in students' personal, family, and community lives for academic learning. Accordingly, R.E.A.L. instruction builds on and further develops adolescent English learners' complete set of literacy skills.

Language is one of the funds of knowledge that English learners already possess (Mercado, 2005); consequently, literacy does not only refer to how we come to know something in English. We should consider literacy in relation to students' full linguistic repertoire, with a focus on bilingualism. Students already possess language skills (written, oral, or both) that are incredible assets that we should build on for their **biliteracy** development. Escamilla and colleagues (2014) explain that biliteracy is the ability to read, write, and perform other literacy tasks in more than one language. Certainly, ELs, by definition, will be developing literacy in English, but they should also have the opportunity to cultivate first language development in all **language domains**—reading, writing, listening, and speaking.

Most adolescent ELs will not be in official bilingual classrooms where a language other than English will be a formal language of whole-class instruction (Menken, 2013). They are most often in **English-medium classrooms**, where English is the primary language of curriculum and instruction and the teacher does not necessarily speak the students' first language. In these classes, the stated goals determined by states or school districts are academic achievement and language development in English (García, Johnson, & Seltzer, 2017); nevertheless, an uncompromising principle of R.E.A.L. instruction is to improve students' linguistic abilities in all of their languages so they can reap the benefits of these skills both in and out of the classroom. Chapter 6 explains in more detail how teachers can support students' biliteracy development through R.E.A.L. instruction—even teachers who do not speak students' L1s.

To sum up, *relevant, engaging,* and *affirming literacy* instruction is the focus for all reading and reader response activities shared in this book. Understanding how to apply these principles to a literacy classroom with adolescent ELs requires that we fully understand our students beyond the labels we give them.

WHO ARE ADOLESCENT ENGLISH LEARNERS?

Though they do not fully represent the students, labels are what we use to refer to different learner populations. Though they are useful to an extent, we need to understand the limitations of the label *English learner* that is widely used to describe the students who are the focus of this book. The term

English learner, often used synonymously with *English language learner* or *ELL*, makes languages other than English that the student possesses invisible (García et al., 2017). R.E.A.L. instruction, in contrast to the assumptions inherent with the term *EL*, explicitly highlights these other rich languages; in fact, R.E.A.L. instruction seeks to value, leverage, and develop students' languages in addition to English while also providing instruction for effective English language acquisition.

Many in the field of bilingual education research have argued for a more accurate name for students who are learning English in our schools (Chappel & Faltis, 2013; Menken, 2013; Valdés, Menken, & Castro, 2015.) The term **emergent bilingual** (García & Kleifgen, 2010) is often used to refer to ELs and takes an asset-perspective, highlighting what students have—bilingual abilities—rather than what they do not yet have—namely, English proficiency to the degree needed to accomplish grade-level academic tasks in English. Although I generally prefer the term *emergent bilingual*, I have chosen to use *EL* in this book instead because I recognize that it is the term most commonly used, along with *ELL*, within the literacy field, and even more so within adolescent literacy (e.g., Beach, Appleman, Fecho, & Simon, 2016). Though I have made the difficult decision to use the term *English learner*, my view is that focal students in this book are multilingual, multiliterate, and multicultural transnational global citizens. Know that every time you read the term *EL* in the book, all of the asset-based labels are the lens through which I view these students and the lens I hope teachers of R.E.A.L. instruction will adopt.

In addition to labeling limitations, it is also important to highlight the diversity within the population of students who are learning English in secondary classrooms. This book is focused on teaching all ELs from all language backgrounds and English proficiency levels, recognizing that adolescent ELs are actually a very diverse population. Certainly, students in the dynamic process of language acquisition are diverse at any level, but middle and high school teachers see even more diversity in their ELs as a result of the greater amount of time students have had to live different experiences (Menken, 2013). Although a myriad of factors account for the diversity of adolescent ELs, four are, in my experience, the most pertinent to our instructional decisions: students' English proficiency level, prior education, experiences with language, and time in the new country.

English Proficiency Level

Various organizations, researchers, and governmental agencies, including WIDA and TESOL (Teacher of English to Speakers of Other Languages), have developed descriptors to describe one's second language **(L2)** proficiency. Additionally, many researchers use these organizations' terminology or modifications of it to describe an EL's performance in different language domains (e.g., Honigsfeld & Dove, 2013; Wright, 2010). Most of us tend to discuss ELs' language proficiency in English according to the way our state or region requires us to classify students' performance, meaning we do not necessarily share a common language to converse about this crucial piece of knowledge for teaching students. I appreciate the descriptive and asset-oriented WIDA terminology (WIDA, 2015), but for the purposes of this book I will use basic descriptors of students' overall second language proficiency that are easily understandable for those who are accustomed to various descriptors or none at all: *beginner*, *intermediate*, and *advanced*. However, it is extremely important that as you begin planning R.E.A.L. instruction for your ELs, you determine more specifically what students *can* do in each language domain—reading, writing, listening, and speaking. If you are not already using a classification system to understand your ELs' specific abilities, I suggest that you use WIDA's rubrics, available online at https://www.wida.us/standards/eld.aspx, to assess each one of your unique students in order to plan instruction and appropriate supports in the classroom. This knowledge should be one of the main factors in guiding your classroom decisions for students' reading and responding activities.

Prior Education and Schooling in the L1

Some ELs in our classrooms will not have had prior educational experiences in any country or will have had extremely limited formal schooling. Although this in no way diminishes the richness of their lived experiences, these students will probably face many challenges when they come to our secondary classrooms. These students might be labeled SIFE (**Students with Interrupted Formal Education**) or SLIFE (**Students with Limited or Interrupted Formal Education**) (DeCapua, Smathers, & Tang, 2007; WIDA, 2015). Many of these students will come to the United States with refugee status and might have experienced years without the opportunity to participate in formal education (Klein & Martohardjono, 2006). Other students might have attended a school without interruptions, but they may have had very poor-quality education. The point is that these students (SIFES or SLIFES) are not able to engage in age-appropriate (according to the new country's standards) print-based literacy in any language. However, with appropriate instruction that provides them with the literacy skills they need to learn, they can thrive academically (Stewart, 2015, 2016, 2017). It is crucial that we refrain from taking a deficit view of students with limited learning opportunities with labels such as *preliterate* or *illiterate*. All students have some form of language and literacy abilities, the means to send and receive meaning, and it is our job to recognize those strengths in order to build on them. However, I have made the mistake of handing a student a book in her first language, expecting her to read it with ease, when she possessed oral literacy in that language but could not read. By doing this, I only reinforced in her mind what she did not know. Thus, we need to be aware that providing some students with a bilingual dictionary or reading material in their L1 might not be very helpful and may even make students feel more discouraged if we assume that these resources will help them without any further intervention.

Other students will have adequate and even very strong educations in their home countries and can highly benefit from dictionaries, electronic translators, or other materials in their first language. They might possess grade-level (or even above) literacy skills in their first languages, providing a strong foundation for their success; however, despite their advantages, they might feel lost in their new learning environment. I have worked with students who were at the top of their classes in their home countries, and the sudden transition to a new language made them feel like they did not know anything in their classes in English, causing them to question their identity as a learner. Acknowledging these students' abilities in their first language is important, as is remembering that what they can express in a second language such as English does not in any way demonstrate their full knowledge base.

For students with reading and writing abilities in their L1s, it will be important to determine whether their first languages use the same alphabet as English and if they are familiar with the English letter/sound correspondence. Some students might write a language that does not use letters, but rather symbols, in written communication such as Chinese, whereas other students might be familiar with the letter/sound concept but know an alphabet different from the Roman alphabet, as in Russian. Students who speak languages that use the same alphabet as English and where the letter often makes similar sounds, particularly Spanish, will be at an advantage in their beginning English development. We need to capitalize on the language similarities and provide appropriate supports where great differences between the languages exist. For example, I assisted in the classroom of a high school history teacher who had the English alphabet above the board, as is common in elementary classrooms. Two newcomer students who spoke Russian told me that because their alphabet was different, they regularly looked above the board for assistance when looking up English vocabulary in their bilingual dictionaries. The teacher's knowledge about their alphabet and provision of this support assisted these young men as they engaged in grade-level vocabulary exercises.

Long-term English learners (LTELs) are students who have attended U.S. schools and received English as a second language services for over 5 years, but have not demonstrated adequate progress on English language and content-area assessments because they might struggle with **academic language** (Freeman, Mercuri, & Freeman, 2001). We must reflect on why these students have not progressed in their second language acquisition as demonstrated by the assessments we use. Valenzuela's (1999) notion of **subtractive schooling**, an education that has divested them of their language and cultural resources for years, merits our consideration because many LTELs did not have access to an early education that allowed them to develop L1 literacy skills. Furthermore, Valenzuela's (1999) research illustrates how failing to recognize and leverage students' cultures in the classroom can have a negative effect on their learning. Subtractive schooling does not see students or value their cultural and linguistic resources, stealing their greatest assets for literacy and academic learning.

Similarly, researchers of bilingualism have illustrated the literacy and academic losses when students are not provided with foundational education in their native languages (e.g., Collier & Thomas, 2009). If the students we label LTELs have been in the United States for their early education, they might not have had access to high-quality bilingual programs that provided them with the opportunity to develop a strong foundation in their first language while learning in an environment that connected to their culture.

Unfortunately, long-term ELs are often compared to newcomers who have had the benefit of receiving a robust academic foundation in their first language and can therefore leverage those cognitive benefits for further academic and language learning. We should be quick to acknowledge these newcomers' strong foundation in L1 literacy, which allows them to reap the benefits of that education while they are acquiring English. Their previous schooling experiences gave them full access to the curriculum in the language they spoke at home and mirrored their family's cultural values, setting them up for academic success for the remainder of their lives. Therefore, we must understand that they might progress more quickly than long-term English learners who might have experienced the negative consequences of subtractive schooling. As educators of both groups of students, we should be careful of narratives that place blame on LTELs themselves for their academic struggles and not simply compare their English progress as demonstrated on exams to the progress of their peers who are newer to the country.

Additionally, we need to see long-term ELs' strengths and how they use language in complex ways to make meaning (Brooks, 2016) that might not be valued on the assessments by which they are evaluated. R.E.A.L. instruction provides an opportunity to meet students where they are and take an asset-oriented stance to the literacies they already possess. Some studies have shown the benefits of attending to the language loss that occurs in subtractive schooling by developing LTELs' first languages while supporting them in English language development at the secondary level (Menken & Kleyn, 2010; Olsen, 2010). R.E.A.L. instruction provides a way for teachers to support all students' L1 development regardless of the opportunities they have or have not had in the past.

Time in New Country's Schools

Secondary students who are new to the country and, by default, the country's schools are sometimes referred to as *late arrivals* (Salinas, 2006) because most of their schooling is completed in other countries. This term emphasizes the students' limited time to acquire sufficient English to receive the credits and pass the tests required to receive a high school diploma in particular states. We also use the label *newcomer* (Short & Boyson, 2012) for the same students to emphasize their newness in a given country. If these students have not been exposed to English previously in their home countries, they will be at the beginning stages of English acquisition, and their progress will be dependent on other factors from their past, such as L1 development and previous schooling.

Other ELs are what I call *on-time language acquirers.* These students, who might have been in the new country's schools for 2 or 3 years, often come to me lamenting that they cannot pass a state test or are struggling to read a novel or textbook in another class. Most recently, Yadira, a student from Puerto Rico in her second year in the United States, came to me with tears in her eyes, showing me the letter from the school stating that she had failed the state exams. These exams are designed for native English speakers, and in the year I had worked with her, I had noted her excellent English language progress. I thought if she continued, she would be able to perform well on that test in a year or two. Sometimes this occurs with a similar student who feels downtrodden because he cannot comprehend a reading assignment given to native English-speakers with no additional supports. I tell them: "You're not supposed to be able to read that novel independently without support or pass that test anyway because it takes time to learn a second language." Some research suggests it might take 5 to 7 years or even longer for a student in a supportive second language acquisition environment to obtain grade-level academic skills in the second language (Baker, 2011; Cummins, 1979).

Thus, we have ELs in our class who may have been learning English in our schools for 3 years and are at an intermediate level. Whereas some states' expectations might be for students to advance a level indicator or more each year, an intermediate indicator (whether the term is actually *intermediate, developing,* or a number) might be a very natural place for students to be in their second language acquisition. These students, while perhaps being labeled EL for a few years, might be right on track for acquiring advanced communication and academic skills in their second language. Our job is to further their language acquisition while assuring them that they are progressing well on the long journey of second language acquisition despite test scores that may be overwhelmingly discouraging and defeating. Further along the continuum of time in the country's schools, long-term ELs might have been born in an English-speaking country or lived there most of their lives, which explains their fluency in conversational English despite their struggle with more academically demanding English language tasks. Regardless of whether our students have attended schools in our country for anywhere from 10 days to 10 years, we need to possess basic knowledge of second language acquisition research if we hope to be their advocates with their other teachers, administrators, parents, and even policymakers.

In short, before we can effectively select instructional tools that will be relevant or engaging to students, affirm them, or take an asset-oriented stance toward their literacy practices, we need to understand our ELs— the richness and diversity of their experiences, language use, strengths, and obstacles. This is an ongoing process that can start before you meet your students and continue long after they have left your classroom. One way to take the first steps to prepare yourself for R.E.A.L. instruction is to begin reading literature that might allow you to walk in your students' shoes to a certain extent. Table 1.1 provides literature that I recommend for developing an understanding of some of your future or current students. I do not imply that the books mentioned in this table cover the full range of ELs' experiences; however, they have taught me a great deal about the experiences of many students I had the opportunity to know.

PURPOSE OF THE BOOK

It is evident that the people this book is about, adolescent English learners, are vastly heterogeneous and deserve both our study of them and the kind of instruction that benefits them. As a result, the purpose of this book is to describe R.E.A.L. instruction for middle and high school **English as a Second Language (ESL)** and **English language arts (ELA)** teachers who are teaching adolescent ELs at all levels of English acquisition and in both homogeneous groupings and multileveled classrooms. To illustrate, R.E.A.L. instruction is for the ESL teacher with a roomful of middle school newcomers as well as the ELA teacher who has only two ELs within her mainstream senior English classroom. This book is for teachers in dual-credit, advanced placement, honors, developmental, or credit compensation classes. Additionally, a teacher of a middle or high school reading class, after-school book club, or summer literacy course can apply this instruction.

Furthermore, the teacher of R.E.A.L. instruction does not need to be bilingual, although I learned Spanish as a second language as a young adult. While my second language learning has given me firsthand knowledge of the second language acquisition experience and my knowledge of the Spanish language is often an asset, R.E.A.L. instruction does not require a bilingual teacher. Many of the teachers I work with do not speak their students' languages, and I have worked with many youth whose languages I do not speak. Though I encourage all teachers to gain awareness of what it is like to develop literacy in a second language by becoming language learners themselves, R.E.A.L. instruction is for all ESL or ELA teachers, regardless of the languages they do or do not speak.

Through this book, I want to provide literacy educators with rich descriptions of successful practices in the secondary classroom with students who are adding English to their linguistic repertoires while acknowledging teachers' professional autonomy to make the most effective curricular and instructional decisions for their students. In describing how teachers facilitate various literacy activities with multileveled students, my hope is to let the reader decide what is applicable in other settings and with other students. Because literacy instruction occurs with diverse students in various learning environments led by teachers who have different strengths, there cannot be a one-size-fits-all

Table 1.1. Books for Teachers to Read to Understand Adolescent English Learners' Experiences

Book	Topics Covered	Additional Information
Castilla, J. M. (2009). *Strange parents.* Houston, TX: Piñata Books.	Family separation and reunification	Novel Fiction
Cofer, J. O. (2004). *Call me María: A novel.* New York, NY: Orchard Books.	Learning English Family separation Fitting in	Novel in verse Fiction
Ho, M. (2003). *The stone goddess.* New York, NY: Orchard Books.	Surviving war and trauma Refugee experience	Novel Historical fiction
*Medina, J., & Casilla, R. (2004). *The dream on Blanca's wall: Poems in English and Spanish.* Honesdale, PA: Wordsong/Boyds Mills Press.	Making dreams Breaking stereotypes	Poems
*Medina, J., & Vanden Broeck, F. (1999). *My name is Jorge on both sides of the river: Poems.* Honesdale, PA: Wordsong/Boyds Mills Press.	The importance of one's name The ESL classroom experience	Poems
*Davis, J. (2014). *Spare parts: Four undocumented teenagers, one ugly robot, and the battle for the American dream.* New York, NY: Farrar, Straus, and Giroux.	Overcoming difficulties with immigration Desire to achieve Teacher's role in students' success	Novel Nonfiction Also a movie
Castilla, J. M. (1999). *Emilio.* Houston, TX: Piñata Books.	Learning English Adjusting to a new culture	Novel Fiction
*Nazario, S. (2013). *Enrique's journey: The true story of a boy determined to reunite with his mother.* New York, NY: Delacorte Press.	Unaccompanied minors Central American youth Family separation and reunification	Novel Nonfiction

Table 1.1. Books for Teachers to Read to Understand Adolescent English Learners' Experiences (continued)

*Diaz, A. (2016). *The only road.* New York, NY: Simon & Schuster Books for Young Readers.	Unaccompanied minors Central American youth	Novel Fiction
Fraillon, Z. (2016). *The bone sparrow.* New York, NY: Disney-Hyperion.	Life in a refugee camp/detention center	Novel Fiction
St. John, W. (2012). *Outcasts united: The story of a refugee soccer team that changed a town.* New York, NY: Delacorte Press.	The refugee experience before, during, and after resettlement	Novel Nonfiction
Atkin, S. B. (1993). Fitting in. In S. B. Atkin (Ed.), *Voices from the fields: Children of migrant farmworkers tell their stories* (pp. 36–43). Boston, MA: Little Brown and Company.	ELs from Mexico who speak languages other than Spanish	Informational text taken from an interview
*Grande, R. (2012). *The distance between us: A memoir.* New York, NY: Atria Books.	Childhood in Mexico Parent separation	Novel Memoir
Levine, E., & Björkman, S. (1989). *I hate English!* New York, NY: Scholastic Inc.	Stages of learning English	Picture book Fiction

These books might be appropriate for your students as well depending on the topic, your students' experiences, and the text complexity. *Books available in Spanish

approach. Consequently, I hope that literacy teachers, specialists, and coaches might not only *adopt* these practices, but also *adapt* them in ways that are tailored toward their students through their understanding of related theories and, most important, their understanding of their unique students.

The teaching and learning descriptions in this book represent relevant, engaging, and affirming literacy instruction that took place in actual classrooms—multileveled classrooms of students with teachers who face the same challenges of standardization and testing as you do today. The practices described in this book are also based on significant theory, yet often, theory and practice are in contention, particularly regarding teaching secondary ELs (Menken, 2013). For example, Menken (2013) recognizes that there is convincing research support for building on ELs' home language and literacy practices in order to further their academic success as measured in English; however, these L1 skills are rarely even acknowledged at the secondary level.

Consequently, some instructional suggestions based on theory and practice in this book might push the envelope of what is considered traditional middle or high school English instruction—instruction that does not take into account students' L1. Deviating from tradition, R.E.A.L. instruction takes theory to practice, signifying that practitioners should understand the theoretical framework behind specific instructional and curricular decisions to privilege student learning above the way things have always been done, conventional wisdom based on monolingual principles, or narrowly defined learning outcomes.

THEORY SUPPORTING R.E.A.L. INSTRUCTION

A warm, welcoming attitude about English learners and an understanding of their experiences is not enough. These students' education and future as productive citizens is in our hands. Their success is inextricably linked to the success of our nation (Suárez-Orozco, Suárez-Orozco, & Todorova, 2008); hence, we need to expertly apply research from various fields in order to provide our students with the most effective instruction.

The ESL or ELA classroom teacher with diverse students who are simultaneously acquiring English language, literacy skills, and content knowledge has many instructional elements to consider. Therefore, R.E.A.L. instruction draws from three main areas of research: (1) reader response theory, highlighting the importance of reading and responding to literature; (2) second language acquisition, acknowledging a prime need of English learners to acquire English; and (3) bilingual theory, to understand how learners' multiple languages interact and support one another.

Reader Response Theory

Reader response entails how one reacts (or transacts [Rosenblatt, 1978]) to/with a piece of literature. In this book, I specifically use the term to denote what one does before, during, and after reading, including the thinking, speaking, writing, and creating that represent responses to the literature. One of the best-known scholars in reader response theory is Louise Rosenblatt (1940, 1978) who encouraged teachers to consider the lived experiences that students bring with them to any reading and to include contemporary literature with the classics in order to connect to the reader's experiences. By challenging a single understanding of a literary work, Rosenblatt highlighted how we interpret what we read based on our own unique set of experiences. The unique transaction between the text and the reader is what Rosenblatt (1978) called "the poem." She did not want students to read in order to merely analyze, memorize, or get the correct answer; rather, she encouraged a "living through" (2005) of literature and invited us to set the conditions needed for that to occur within our classrooms. Living through literature is a foundational principle of R.E.A.L. instruction, and much of this book will explore how to facilitate the living through experience for our adolescent ELs as they transact with texts.

First, we must consider the reading material we provide our students both in and out of the classroom. What genres do we give them? What cultures are represented by the content, illustrations, and authors of the books? In what languages are the books written? Whose stories are worthy of being in print? Which authors really count? R.E.A.L. instruction calls for us to continually evaluate our classroom bookshelves and assignments with a critical eye.

Many scholars highlight the importance of providing students with literature in which they see their lived experiences reflected (Brooks, 2006; Sims, 1983; Sutherland, 2005)—texts that connect to their identities. Rudine Sims's (1983) work on reader response from a cultural perspective is particularly appropriate for R.E.A.L. instruction. She introduces us to Osula, an African American girl who responded positively to texts with strong Black female characters who had experiences similar to her own. Through metaphor, she asks us to consider if literature is a *window* or a *mirror* for students (Sims Bishop, 1990). A window permits students to see into other worlds, which is very influential, facilitating their entrance into previously unimagined places. Yet Sims (1983) reminds us of the power of mirrors, which allow our own lived experiences to be reflected back to us. Throughout this book, I highlight the importance of purposefully providing adolescent ELs with mirror experiences in literature while also giving them opportunities to enter new worlds through windows.

Brooks and Browne (2012) call for a culturally situated reader response theory that I think is particularly significant for adolescent English learners. In this theory, the reader will take up a dominant cultural position while reading literature termed the **Homeplace Position**, which is influenced by one's community, ethnic group, peers, and family. The Homeplace Position is still influenced by other Supporting Positions such as popular culture and the views of other cultural groups that live in the same society. Brooks and Browne (2012) explain:

> The Homeplace Position represents the most dominant perspective being evoked when a child offers a literary response. This position remains transient and constantly interacts with and gets informed by the other positions. The Supporting Positions continue to be influential to a student's response, but they are not as focal. (p. 78)

These positions are dynamic and fluid, and they influence one another. Although the students' responses will primarily be determined by the Homeplace Position in which they identify with the text in culturally specific ways, outside influences are also at play. Nevertheless, it is the reader's experiences, the heart of his or her own culture, that provide a lens used to make meaning from the text as the reader relates to it. Ways that students can personally relate to the text may be referred to as "cultural access points that . . . enable a story to resonate and become meaningful for them" (Brooks & Browne, 2012, p. 83). The more access points a text provides a reader, which can occur through connections to the reader's lived experiences, cultural traditions, or interests, the more the meaningful or comprehensible the story might become to him or her.

This explains why some research suggests that English learners will more effectively develop reading skills and find meaning in a text when they can relate to the characters or the experiences in the book (Araujo, 2013; Ebe, 2012; Giouroukakis & Honigsfeld, 2010; Stewart, 2015). When they have more connections to the experiences of the characters, they have more affordances (Van Lier, 2000) to make meaning from the words on the page. This is particularly crucial for students reading in their second language to acquire content and language knowledge.

Second Language Acquisition Theory

Adolescent ELs all share the need to acquire English; thus, various components in second language acquisition theory are also relevant to R.E.A.L. instruction. Indeed, vocabulary development is one of the greatest challenges for ELs, particularly in secondary schools, because in only a few years, they need to acquire the vocabulary in English that other students have spent years acquiring both in and out of school (Wright, 2010). In addition to word knowledge, students also need a strong understanding of grammatical structures and syntax in English to be academically successful on assessments designed for native English speakers that ELs in some states must pass in order to graduate high school (Menken, 2008; Stewart, 2014). Not possessing the vocabulary knowledge or structural understanding of English needed to understand multiple-choice questions, writing prompts, and reading passages can prove very frustrating to these students, and we need to understand how best to support their second language development.

Whereas it is only a small part of the large body of research in second language acquisition, below I highlight particular aspects of the learning environment that Ortega (2009) explains are crucial components for optimal language growth. First, we should consider the learner's attitude toward the culture of the target language or L2—in this case, English. This suggests the need to help students in the **acculturation** process; that is, encouraging their ties to their home culture while helping them process aspects of their new culture. Adolescents need to know you not are pushing them toward **assimilation**, to have their culture replaced by the dominant culture, or to become similar to their native-born classmates. Forced assimilation can lead to a negative attitude toward the English language. English acquisition will optimally occur when they are encouraged to maintain ties to their own culture while adopting the cultural practices of their new country at their own pace.

The second ingredient of the optimal language learning environment is **comprehensible input** (Krashen, 1994). Input entails what the student hears from classmates or the teacher as well as what the student reads or views. English acquisition will occur most effectively when that input is comprehensible. To illustrate, think of text you have seen in another language. Sometimes the text is accompanied by a visual, which helps us understand it; however, a full page of text in a language in which we do not have proficiency might not mean anything to us. We have to consider whether the text we give students is comprehensible and what we need to do in order to make a given text intelligible.

Related to comprehensible input is the place where second language acquisition can most effectively occur, at what Krashen (1994) refers to as the $i + 1$ level. This is the individual's (i) level of second language proficiency plus one ($+ 1$), or a text containing just a few words and grammatical structures in which the reader is not fully competent yet. In that way, the students are gaining exposure to new words, grammatical structures, idioms, or other phrases, yet they understand the context well enough to make sense of what is new. Comprehensible input might also occur through listening and viewing, which are also most effective at the $i + 1$ level for English acquisition.

This connects well to culturally situated reader response theory, which suggests that the more connections a student has to a text, the more meaningful and comprehensible it will be (Brooks & Browne, 2012). Nonetheless, if I were given a novel in Russian that connected to my lived experiences, it would still be incomprehensible because my individual level of Russian language knowledge is extremely limited. For second language acquisition to effectively occur, we should consider the learner's Homeplace Position (Brooks & Browne, 2012) as well as his or her individual level of English language proficiency. The goal is to give students literature that is at the $i + 1$ level, not the $i + 25$ level, even if the book is on "the list" or is part of the revered literary canon.

As students read comprehensible texts while developing positive attitudes about English and their new culture, they also need to respond, or produce output (Ortega, 2009). Swain (1985) discusses **pushed output**: speaking or writing that demands more of the learner than he or she is currently able to produce easily. This calls for inviting ELs to take risks as they respond to their reading through writing or speaking; however, we need to provide **scaffolding**, or appropriate temporary supports, for these risks in order to help students be successful in their risk-taking in English production. This requires that we provide them with varied and appropriate response activities that include language supports and creative ways to express their learning. In short, reading (input) alone is not sufficient for optimal second language learning; we must also expect students to produce responses in order to give them the best atmosphere to acquire English (Ortega, 2009).

The notions of input and output are related to a fourth component of the optimal second language acquisition environment that Ortega (2009) identifies, **negotiated interaction**. Long (1996) explains that the ideal comprehensible input for the L2 learners is interactionally modified. For example, a teacher might look for signals that the EL needs more support in understanding a text or oral language, which could include a questioning look on the student's face, zoning out, or the obvious "Huh?" As the teacher receives this feedback, the next set of inputs can be modified through rephrasing, slower speech, visual and aural cues (the written with the spoken word), L1 support, or directly explaining certain vocabulary or sentence structures that are causing confusion. This process involves regular opportunities for students to clarify the input and confirm their comprehension. Therefore, a teacher might insert regular clarification checks into English instruction that can occur in any language.

Finally, Ortega (2009) includes an attention to language code as a fifth component of the effective SLA environment that might excite grammar enthusiasts because it implies that ELs need to move beyond **communicative competence**, defined as speaking or writing to be understood and understand others. They need an environment that will cause them to pay attention to the **language code**, its grammar rules and conventions, in a manner that does not diminish their output and willingness to take risks. This is where the art of teaching comes in, as too much attention to the language code for students too early can cause them to shut down or produce less output for fear of making an error. (Think of the student who cleverly writes the least amount possible to avoid losing points for written mistakes.) However, ELs need regular guidance on both oral and written language codes. Much of this will be discussed in response activities throughout the book as teachers provide appropriate scaffolding for ELs' speaking and writing in English through various strategies.

Although not part of Ortega's (2009) five crucial components for second language learning, extremely pertinent to the premise of R.E.A.L. instruction is Krashen's (2004) assertion that pleasurable reading, or what he calls *free voluntary reading*, is a key component of academic vocabulary acquisition in the second language and more effective than direct instruction. **Free voluntary reading** entails students selecting what they want to read in the second language to engage in **sustained silent reading**. Krashen (2012) further argues that the only way students will develop the vocabulary they need to meet the rigorous demands placed on them in their second language is to engage in large amounts of reading that is enjoyable and self-selected.

Bilingual Theory

Reader response and second language acquisition research provide a strong foundation for teaching adolescent ELs, yet we would be remiss to ignore students' first or home languages, which are also important in providing them with appropriate reading and reader response activities. Research indicates that students' first languages can be systematically leveraged to support their English language development (Cook, 2001; Cummins, 2007; Martínez, 2010) and that literacy skills and knowledge learned in one language can transfer to another (Cummins, 2000). Even if students are not placed in a classroom officially designated as bilingual, ELs are multilinguals who cannot be viewed through a monolingual lens.

Consequently, García (2008) calls for a **multilingual awareness pedagogy** for all teachers, not just those with the official title of ESL or bilingual educators. She maintains that although schooling in the United States and Europe has traditionally ignored students' multiple languages at the secondary level, a school with even one bilingual student becomes a multilingual school. Therefore, any teacher of ELs should possess not just a deep knowledge of the English language, but also an understanding of pedagogy that incorporates students' bilingualism in the classroom. García (2008) claims that a multilingual awareness pedagogy can transform teachers' practice and students' lives through its empowering nature as we see the assets students bring with them into our classrooms, rather than just their need to learn English.

Although this book will not attempt to fully understand or analyze adolescent ELs' bilingualism, it is important for us to consider a more fluid view of bilingualism that includes our bilingual students' **translanguaging** practices (García & Li Wei, 2014)—how, why, and for what purposes they use their multiple languages. Translanguaging[2], or drawing across all one's languages in order to make meaning, is a practice in which bilinguals regularly engage and that all teachers should understand and systematically leverage in order to effectively teach students who have communication abilities in more than one language (García et al., 2017). Translanguaging entails students using English as well as their home language(s) to send and receive meaning through oral or written communication. Many researchers are now considering how students' multiple languages interact with one another and how we can capitalize on this phenomenon in the academic setting, particularly with adolescents (Daniel & Pacheco, 2016; García, Flores, & Chu, 2011; Stewart & Hansen-Thomas, 2016).

Through this view, ELs are positioned as bilinguals whose languages do not exist separately. They fluidly move back and forth between their languages, which provide them with what García (2009) compares to an all-terrain vehicle (ATV). This means that bilinguals, such as the ELs in your class, have the adaptability for different communicative situations: They can learn to make strategic language decisions to accomplish specific goals in a variety of

2. I acknowledge that a translanguaging pedagogy does not entail language designations such as L1 or L2 (García & Kleyn, 2016). However, for the practical purposes of this book in considering how best to teach students acquiring English in the secondary ELA or ESL classroom, the distinctions between one's first and second language seem to be appropriate for determining curriculum and instructional practices.

settings. This is surely an asset for our bilingual students, yet they need practice and instruction in how to operate this powerful tool, and we, as English
educators, can provide them with that guidance by increasing our knowledge
base about bilingualism, not necessarily by learning each student's first language. Indeed, addressing how theory regarding translanguaging can systematically guide practices in the ELA class is "a matter of affirmative action"
(Canagarajah, 2011, p. 2) and "social justice" (García et al., 2017), highlighting the need for all teachers to understand how students' multiple languages interact in order to most effectively teach them literacy and language.

EXPERIENCES SUPPORTING R.E.A.L. INSTRUCTION

In addition to the theory presented above and throughout this book that has
nurtured the implementation of R.E.A.L. instruction, my time with actual
students both in and out of the classroom has influenced what I believe is
an effective approach for teaching ELs in the literacy learning environment.
Thus, the work in this book comes from a compilation of my experiences
attempting to put theory into practice in ways that most benefit students.
First, I was a 6th-grade ESL teacher for newcomer youth in a special public
middle/high school that only served students in their first year in the United States. Because I was a novice teacher (and human), I surely made many
mistakes, yet I can look back and recognize that I might have done a few
things right—specifically, providing students with large amounts of literature
choices in English and their L1s, while allotting class time for independent
reading. I also spent time with these middle school newcomers outside of
class, learning their stories and laying the foundation to see them as unique
individuals.

More recently, the practices described in this book come from various
teacher–researcher experiences in high school ESL or ELA classrooms with
students who are learning English. Sometimes I am a participant–observer
in English classrooms where I observe how ELs react to the curriculum and
instruction in their class and then assist them with their assignments. I sit at
their tables, write in my journal when they do, and participate in their group-
work. I also spend much time with these same students outside of class,
interviewing them about their experiences to understand literacy and language instruction from their perspective. At other times, I work alongside the
teacher to make instructional innovations to the curriculum, primarily using
literature and reader response activities that will be effective for students at all
levels of English acquisition in these multilevel classrooms. We try different
techniques to teach students as a whole class although their second language
levels vary greatly, and other times, we divide them up into groups based on
interests, first languages, or English proficiency. In some classrooms, I get
to become the visiting teacher and teach the entire class or regularly lead
small groups of students in book clubs within their English classes. These

experiences occur at all points in the school year, even during testing season, in both ESL (elective) and ELA (credit) classrooms. The excellent teachers to whom I introduce you in this book are Marie, Kelly, and Susan, all high school ELA and ESL teachers who represent various levels of experience and knowledge of second language acquisition. They teach multileveled classes, illustrating the accessibility of R.E.A.L. instruction.

Although these teachers and I have implemented R.E.A.L. instruction during the school year, I have the most fun conducting summer literacy institutes with classes of refugee and immigrant youth. This gives me an environment where I can try out new ideas to share later with teachers to use in their own classrooms. However, I purposefully use the activities and texts that seem to work well in the summer during the school year in an environment that might be more constrained by testing, curriculum requirements, or time.

Through these experiences, I recognize that teaching is challenging, particularly teaching diverse students whose educational and language experiences vary greatly. Yet I have also realized that I may have more to learn from adolescent English learners than I have to teach them. Approaching these classrooms as a learner, with my passport ready to travel the world with students through their experiences, is exciting, inspiring, and transformative.

ACTION TIME

- Are you affirming students by saying their name correctly? Take the pledge at www.mynamemyidentity.org.

- Read *René Has Two Last Names* (Colato Laínez & Graullera Ramírez, 2009) or *My Name Is Bilal* (Mobin-Uddin & Kiwak, 2005) with your class to begin discussing their names. Find out what each student's full name is and the meaning of each of their given, middle, and surnames. Learn if these categories even exist in their cultures.

- Learn the following information about your English learners, perhaps involving a translator or their parents. Be very careful not to make the students feel ashamed if they do not have many educational experiences in another country or if they do not know how to read or write in their L1.

  ✓ Place of birth

  ✓ Time in new country and time in home country

  ✓ Previous educational experiences in the new country and other countries

  ✓ Experiences going back and forth between countries

  ✓ What language(s) do they use with parents? Siblings? Friends? In various places in their community?

    ✓ How well can they read and write in languages other than English?

    ✓ Do these languages share the same alphabet as English? Are letters or symbols used in written communication?

    ✓ Do they have books available to them in their first language?

    ✓ How much English language support have they received in the past? What has or has not worked?

- Conduct a bilingual profile of your students as guided by the information in *The Translanguaging Classroom: Leveraging Student Bilingualism for Learning* (García et al., 2017) to understand their proficiency in all of their languages.

- Think about your classroom or a classroom you've observed over the course of a grading period and consider the following questions regarding English learners:

    ✓ What did they read (independently or in class)?

    ✓ Could they make cultural connections with the reading material?

    ✓ Was the content comprehensible and the language accessible?

    ✓ Were students able to use their L1s and develop their bilingualism during this period?

- Read from the selections in Table 1.1 or these texts that share the stories of adolescent English learners to broaden your understanding of the experiences some of them might have:

    ✓ Sadowski, M. (2013). *Portraits of promise: Voices of successful immigrant students.* Cambridge, MA: Harvard Education Press.

    ✓ Stewart, M. A. (2017). *Understanding adolescent immigrants: Moving toward an extraordinary discourse for extraordinary youth.* Lanham, MD: Lexington Books.

- Watch the documentary *I Learn American* (available at ilearnamerica.com) and read some of the stories of the adolescent English learners who have contributed to the human library. Consider their language, literacy, and bilingual strengths and needs.

CHAPTER 2

Set High Expectations
Through R.E.A.L. Instruction

"Tell me about what you are reading," I say to Carlos, a young man in the 10th grade from Puerto Rico who has told me previously he doesn't really like reading—in any language—and regularly writes the bare minimum in his journal when students are asked to respond. His teacher, Marie, and I have started a campaign in his class called "sprint to summer." We are not going to slack off at the end of the year as the weather gets warm, nor will we even have a free day after testing. Literacy learning will happen every day, even on weekends, throughout the school year and, we hope, into the summer. As we begin our "sprint to summer" right before spring break, we expect Carlos and the other students to have at least one self-selected book in their backpack that goes home for reading each afternoon. They have access to a variety of texts in different genres, levels in English, and languages to choose from. If they do not see something they like, they can put in a special request or explain what they might be interested in reading to me so I can try and connect them to something they would find meaningful.

Consequently, my question to Carlos is not, "Have you been reading?" I expect that he is reading and help him select books to read at home, in addition to what he is reading at school with his class. I talk to him about some books I've read and provide some suggestions based on his interests. He ends up with a book of bilingual short stories in English and Spanish; a short book in English about a famous baseball player from his country, Roberto Clemente; and a bilingual illustrated book about Pelé, a well-known soccer player Carlos already knows a lot about because he is a big soccer fan.

Throughout the 10-week campaign, Carlos never reads chapter books in any language at home like others in his class do. He never eagerly seeks me out to tell me what he is reading or to ask for more books on a certain topic. Nor does he bring his journal to me to show me the additional reader response writings he has completed. He is the most reluctant reader in Marie's class for reasons I never fully determine. Unlike other students, he does not work after school or have a high level of family expectations, and although I know reading in English is still difficult for him, he can read well in Spanish. My evaluation of Carlos is that he simply thinks reading is boring, and has not been expected to read outside of school since his arrival in the United

States and perhaps even in Puerto Rico. I also think he was accustomed to always feeling confident, and that confidence has been shaken since moving to the United States with his mother a year and a half ago. He misses his country, the place where he felt at home with his dad and cousins, and he is not completely in control of the decision for him to live in a new place. He deals with separation from the familiar by playing soccer—something he enjoys and feels successful doing, unlike reading. Yet, when expected to read, even for just a few weeks, Carlos reads the books I helped him select—every one of them—with engagement and solid comprehension as evidenced by my weekly conversations with him. My hope is that with the same high expectations month after month, year after year, Carlos will develop a love of reading, in both English and Spanish, which will help him further develop his second language and biliteracy skills, providing him with more opportunities for his future.

NOTHING LESS THAN RIGOROUS STANDARDS

R.E.A.L. instruction is not watered down in any way. I do not feel sorry for Carlos or other students like him who have great gains to make in English, although I know they have mountains to climb and I am realistic about the journey ahead of them. However, because they are the bilingual, biliterate, and bicultural global citizens who need to be in positions of influence for the future, they need rigor in the curriculum and instruction they receive in class.

Rigorous standards do not mean you need to hand readers who are relatively new to the English language works by Shakespeare and Twain and expect deep analytical essays in English with little assistance. Beers and Probst (2013) provide an excellent explanation of rigor, one I think is particularly applicable when considering English learners in secondary ELA classrooms: "Rigor is not an attribute of a text but rather a characteristic of our behavior with the text. . . . [It] resides in the energy and attention given to the text, not the text itself" (p. 20). The authors continue to draw our attention to how an ill-conceived notion of rigor has become "rigor mortis" for our students. From my experience, this is true for many secondary students in the ELA classroom, but this is multiplied increasingly when this same erroneous idea of rigor is applied to students like Carlos.

In addition to considering how we invite students to engage with texts, rigor for ELs might require different supports and materials from those used for native English speakers who are learning in their first language. Gibbons (2009) refers to this as "a high-challenge, high-support" (p. 152) classroom where teachers use a variety of strategies that will be mentioned in this book to make the content comprehensible and meaningful to students. Although we should maintain certain curricular standards, we should not expect the same literacy performance from English learners that we anticipate from monolingual English speakers—we should expect more. When taking the stance of viewing ELs as bilinguals, we should expect them to develop advanced literacy skills in at least two languages, providing them with agency in their present lives and futures (García & Kleyn, 2016).

Although Carlos desperately wants to return to his home in Puerto Rico, he knows that being completely bilingual and biliterate in English and Spanish will greatly benefit him in either country. I can even get him to admit that when he achieves his stated goal of becoming a famous professional soccer player, he can advance his career and have a richer personal life if he possesses more language skills. While I tell him that I support his career goal of becoming the Puerto Rican Pelé, I also want him to discover unimagined possibilities for his future as a successful citizen who is empowered to effect change in his world.

Rigor is also manifested in our classrooms as we expect ELs to tackle issues of discrimination and injustice with keen insight and new perspectives that some non-ELs might not possess. While reading a book (*Sylvia & Aki*, [Conkling, 2011]) on segregation in Marie's class, Carlos, who identifies as a Black Latino, holds out his arm and asks me and a student from Mexico to do the same, representing three distinct skin tones. He profoundly and critically states, "So we could not have been in the same school together." He made connections to his reading and then expressed his critical evaluation of historical events. All ELs should be making these critical connections to the classroom content on a daily basis, and doing it in multiple languages. Carlos's learning went even deeper as his class learned about slavery and he engaged in discussion about how this still affects our world today. As a young Black man, he has insights that some of his friends from Mexico do not have, and the class is able to compare his experiences with those of his Black African friend from the Democratic Republic of the Congo, who sits next to him in class. In Texas, Carlos is often mistaken for a native-English-speaking African American, and at school, some students assume he is from Mexico because he speaks Spanish. His perspectives on issues of discrimination, race, and language from a historical and modern-day context are brought to the surface, challenged, and refined through his teacher's invitation to rigorously engage with text.

I anticipate that English learners will begin to appreciate listening to different perspectives and learning from one another, while always evaluating their stance on an issue and grappling with complex ideas. There are students from three different countries at Carlos's table in his English class. When I show up to learn with them, there are four countries represented. Even just a basic "turn and talk" activity becomes an intersection of multiple worlds and experiences coming together, providing more opportunities for Carlos to hone his evaluation skills and global perspectives. This can and does occur as his teacher provides accessible texts, writing support, and purposeful second language development.

Because our world needs the strengths that English learners can provide, there are no "pobrecitos" in R.E.A.L. instruction (Murillo, 2016) or anthems of "it's just not fair" from good-hearted and well-meaning teachers. Consequently, it is crucial to maintain high standards for your students, expecting them to use literacy for many purposes to accomplish authentic goals. Students need to engage in critical thinking—evaluating ideas, and creatively expressing their own thinking using their full linguistic repertoires in innovative and articulate ways.

NURTURING MULTILINGUAL READERS AND WRITERS AT SCHOOL AND AT HOME

I regularly enter classrooms and tell students that I expect them to read, write, and speak in all of their languages at school and at home. When I mention the "at home" part for the first time, I often get an incredulous "Aw, Miss! Homework?" I talk to them about what they are used to in their classes, and then I can understand why they might think my idea is crazy.

Too many students have become conditioned to view their ESL, developmental reading, or even English language arts classes as the ones without homework. In fact, most secondary ELs tell me that they mainly just have math homework—that is, until R.E.A.L. instruction begins. Perhaps teachers feel that expecting too much in English class is not fair because ELs are too overwhelmed with the content demands of their other core classes. Maybe teachers are cognizant that many of their ELs work after school, help take care of younger siblings, or have multiple responsibilities at home. Or, teachers may have given in to thinking that students just won't read or write outside of school, so there is simply no point in assigning anything.

Yet, I've experienced how expectations can be different. I've seen how teachers can develop relationships with their students, make purposeful changes, and transform the thinking mentioned above that surreptitiously sneaks into our view of students. These views that might come from a place of concern and care for our students ultimately harm their learning and their futures. I also venture that these "no reading and writing at home," low expectations attitudes are harmful to the teacher who misses out on the joy of literacy learning through reading and responding in a global community of learners. I had given in to the system and lost that joy. However, I was able to recover it by staying true to the purposes of R.E.A.L. instruction—literacy, second language, and bilingual development to advanced levels.

THREEFOLD PURPOSE OF R.E.A.L. INSTRUCTION

Teaching students like Carlos can be challenging but it is also exciting and rewarding. Noting his overall literacy development, his English acquisition, and continual growth as a bilingual, biliterate, global citizen makes the hard work well worth the effort.

Literacy Development

First, English learners, like all students, need to further develop their literacy skills in our classes, which include reading and writing in various genres; speaking and listening in multiple registers, dialects, and languages; critical and creative thinking; and using various forms of technology and artistic expression to make meaning (Gibbons, 2009). These multiple literacies are not directly tied to the English language because literacy skills exist and are developed across languages (Cummins, 1979). As an adult with developed reading skills in English, I can certainly transfer those skills to my reading abilities in my second language, Spanish. For example, because I'm adept at using context clues to figure out an unknown word in English, I can use that same skill when I'm reading in Spanish. Likewise, students' ability to use context clues, scan for pertinent information, or find evidence within a text are reading skills that exist outside of a specific language. The skill can manifest itself in any language in which the student possesses adequate proficiency.

Literacy also encompasses skills needed for our students to become responsible citizens in a democracy (Beers & Probst, 2013), including critical thinking, the ability to evaluate an argument, and determine what is fact or fiction and to whom (Cloud, Lakin, Leiniger, & Maxwell, 2010). Subsequently, these skills can be nurtured and developed in any language and we should regularly provide opportunities for students to engage in these high-level processes in all of their languages.

Second Language Development

Literacy development is a primary goal that most English teachers have for all of their students. English learners, however, differ from native English speakers in that they also need to acquire various components of the English language in our classes. Accordingly, another goal for our instruction is to teach elements of the English language such as vocabulary, grammatical structures, and phrases in all language domains.

Reading is a key means of developing English as a second language (Krashen, 2004), which is why we need to purposefully select large quantities of high-quality literature in English for our students to engage with in various ways. As students participate in reading, we need to consider their English language level and how the text supports their second language acquisition.

We should also consider writing and oral language abilities in English in our instruction as we respond to reading. Just as with reading, these reader response activities should be purposeful in taking students to the next level of their English acquisition and using appropriate scaffolding to offer supports for students in reaching that level. Providing students opportunities to read, write, listen, and speak in English is a crucial element of our literacy and language instruction.

Bilingual Development

In order to teach for literacy and language development, we need knowledge in teaching both the language arts and second language acquisition. Most ELA and ESL educators already see themselves as literacy and language teachers. In fact, many see that as complicated enough. Yet, we surely miss out on a crucial element of our students' language resources if we end our instruction there. If we stop with literacy and second language acquisition, we do not really see our students and affirm their bilingual identities. Furthermore, we divest ELs of their greatest learning tool—their home language. If we only see ourselves as literacy and language teachers, we might inadvertently reify the idea that ELs are students who need to become literate and competent in only the English language.

We must remember that ELs are not monolingual, monoliterate, monocultural students. The students I work with are the opposite: multilingual, multiliterate, and multicultural, and we should not deny them access to all of their languages, literacies, and competencies in the classroom. Indeed, all of their languages and their multilingual/multicultural identities can be leveraged for their academic achievement—even their academic achievement that will be measured in English such as on standardized tests. Studies have found that English learners who receive instruction that develops their first language outperform their counterparts who only receive English instruction on academic measurements, even when those assessments are in English (Collier & Thomas, 2009; García & Kleyn, 2016). Therefore, ELA teachers should also be concerned about the bilingual development of their students, seeking to help them further develop literacy in all of their languages, understanding that literacy skills and content knowledge developed in one language will transfer to another, provided sufficient proficiency in that language (Baker, 2011; Cummins, 1979).

Understanding the trifecta (literacy, language, and bilingual development), R.E.A.L. instruction for adolescent English learners draws from multiple theoretical perspectives and research communities—specifically, reader response, second language acquisition, and bilingual education research. Merging these related bodies of work assumes the purposeful stance that adolescent ELs are not only adolescents reading literature. Nor are they only students acquiring a second language or students developing bilingualism. Adolescent ELs are multilingual young adults acquiring literacy and English language skills who need to read and respond to literature that is relevant, engaging, and affirming using their full set of literacy skills while developing even more.

CURRENT CLIMATE: INCREASING DIVERSITY AND STANDARDIZATION

Every secondary literacy educator can benefit from using R.E.A.L. instruction, even in the midst of the current climate of standardization and high-stakes testing. Throughout this book I share literature and reader response activities used in actual secondary ELA and ESL classrooms, all in the environment of standardization within a state with high-stakes testing requirements for graduation.

Certainly, teaching middle or high school language arts is different today from how it was years ago. I am starkly reminded of this as I walk into Marie's high school English I classroom for the first time in what will be my yearlong residency as "the crazy book lady." There is a slide projected on the board that has the word *hello* written in many languages. I look around the room and see the teenagers who speak all of those languages: Chinese, Luganda, French, Lingala, and Spanish. As I get to know students in this class, I realize that even the Spanish speakers represent many countries: Puerto Rico, Honduras, Mexico, Colombia, and Chile. In this class, almost every student is from a different country, and a total of five languages other than English are represented!

You might think this is a special high school for students new to the country. Actually, this is a traditional high school with English learners accounting for only about 5% of the total student population. It is located in the suburbs, where 10 years ago this degree of cultural and linguistic diversity did not exist. These students are pursuing English I credit in a special class for students learning English, and some of the older students are in Marie's mainstream English III class as well—a class with primarily native English speakers. The students who are the newest arrivals are also in Marie's Developmental Reading class—a class dedicated to helping them improve their reading skills and help them pass the state's tests.

Marie, perhaps like you, wears many hats as a teacher of English learners in secondary schools in either mainstream English, **sheltered English** for only ELs, or developmental reading classes. Not long ago, it might have been the task of a special ESL teacher to provide these students with language and literacy instruction. However, nearly every teacher today who wears one of Marie's hats in the classroom is responsible for the language and literacy development of youth in the dynamic process of second language acquisition.

Cultural and linguistic diversity abounds in most classrooms, which calls into question the notion of a mainstream that consists of White, middle-class, native-English-speaking students (Enright, 2011). Indeed, we should modify our perceptions of the secondary ELA classroom to acknowledge the "new mainstream," accepting and celebrating cultural and linguistic diversity as the new standard (Enright, 2011). Surely, this should impact how we instruct students in language (first, second, third, and so on) and literacy (print, digital, and so forth) development. In ELA classrooms today, we are teaching global citizens (Lewis & Dockter, 2011), emergent bilinguals (García & Kleifgen, 2010), transnationals (Skerrett, 2015), and cosmopolitan intellectuals (Campano & Ghiso, 2011) who bring a wealth of knowledge (González et al., 2005) into the literacy learning environment. This diverse population lends itself to a rich and robust atmosphere for exciting literacy and language development.

We might be excited to teach these students as we recognize the vast potential for literacy learning; then, reality sets in. I recognize that, at a time when students' languages, cultures, and lived experiences are growing more wonderfully diverse, curriculum and instruction are (ironically) growing narrower. Teaching in an era of uniformity is difficult for any teacher who believes students should experience literature as they live through each text (Rosenblatt, 1978). However, teaching the language arts is particularly difficult for the English teacher who has increasingly more diverse students coupled with greater standardization. This teacher lives in a paradox—the curriculum and teaching methods are becoming more uniform while the students become more diverse.

We cannot deny that we teach in an era where we might have less professional autonomy than before because standardization accompanies increased accountability through high-stakes testing (W. Au, 2011). This is harmful to the literacy education of all students, but particularly those who are culturally and linguistically diverse—namely, English learners (Menken, 2008; Luke, 2012).

This is dangerous because a monolithic view assumes a uniformity of students that simply does not exist. This view privileges the knowledge of some while ignoring and, by default, devaluing the knowledge of others. What a paradox! Our classrooms contain students who are from different parts of the world, who know different languages (sometimes with different writing systems), who are members of cultural groups with diverse worldviews, whose perspectives often differ from Western thought, whose lived experiences are outside of the country's norm, and whose culturally embedded knowledge is not that of their teachers or those who create our curriculum and assessment tools. Yet, as these richly diverse students enter the language arts classroom, our curriculum, instruction, and evaluation have become more standardized, privileging the assumed norm of monolingualism and monoculturalism.

This is certainly a loss for the students who are in the process of acquiring an L2 as well as multicultural skills. I contend, though, that all students in classes that fail to acknowledge and celebrate diversity, including native English speakers, miss out on cross-cultural learning opportunities and the development of skills needed in the 21st century of global connectedness. ELA teachers are also put in positions of frustration as they need to teach literacy in a way that connects to students' knowledge, yet face restraints within strict standardization regulations. Thus, if we continue onward, failing to make changes in our teaching and curriculum, the English learner, the non-EL students in the classroom, and the teacher all lose, and we should only expect those losses to grow with increasing diversity in the United States as a result of global migration trends.

The Migration Policy Institute (n.d.) estimated that in 2015, 25% or more of children under the age of 18 in the United States had at least one immigrant parent and the vast majority of these children will be exposed to languages other than English at home. Estimates further predict that by 2020, one-third of the school-age population will have an immigrant parent (Mather, 2009). Undoubtedly, the population of English learners in U.S. schools is growing, yet this population growth transcends the elementary classrooms where most professional development and research for teaching ELs is focused (Faltis & Coulter, 2008). More and more ELA teachers in middle and high school are responsible for the literacy and language development of students who are considered English learners.

These students' experiences with language are as diverse as are their lived experiences. It is our responsibility to see, know, and affirm our students in order to effectively teach them (Cummins et al., 2005; Wickstrom et al., 2011). Enright (2011) reminds us that "a well-prepared teacher must have some knowledge of the language backgrounds and cultural experiences of *groups* within his or her classroom but must also learn to attend to the heterogeneity within each group and, indeed, within each individual student" (p. 112). We need to ensure that we are learners of our students and their lives.

Diversity Is Not the Problem

Once we acknowledge the increasing diversity in our classrooms, we need to continually remind ourselves that diversity is not the problem—standardization is. Having diverse students from various countries, cultures, and language backgrounds in our classrooms provides rich soil for transformative learning to take place. Yet, ELA teachers with seven sections of 30 students each, all of whom might be as diverse as Marie's English I students, might think that knowing their students individually in order to provide them with R.E.A.L. instruction is a tall order. Indeed, it can seem daunting, but there is no need to see diversity as a problem. On the contrary, each new layer of diversity that students bring with them into the literacy learning environment only enriches the classroom. Every time a new student arrives in our classroom, we have new learning opportunities available to our community of readers and writers—new ideas to explore and a new cultural insider for a growing body of multicultural literature. For every new EL who arrives in our classroom, the most appropriate attitude should be, "We've been waiting for you to join us."

This is true regardless of the point in the academic year or the high school completion process at which English learners arrive. ELs, more than other student populations, might not always enter our classrooms at what we deem the most appropriate time. They might change schools midyear because of their parents' migratory work in agriculture or transient living, which is common for new immigrants. Neither your students nor their families have control over when economic hardships or war will occur in their countries, prompting emigration to a new country. The United Nations might approve their refugee resettlement in the middle of the U.S. school year. Other students might not have experienced any form of trauma or hardship, but wanted to finish out the school year in their country, which is on a different academic calendar, or they might need to wait until a parent's new job begins or their families' visas are approved. Likewise, once ELs are in your classroom, they cannot control when a death in the family will occur in their country, requiring them to miss days or weeks to travel and be with family. Although it might seem like an interruption to our expert teaching, I can assure you, the adolescent ELs you teach are not trying to disrupt you. The point is, we might need a little perspective to recognize that there are bigger things than our scope and sequence charts.

English learners come to you full of much potential and promise, and our first job is to welcome them. Thus, R.E.A.L. instruction allows for flexibility and spontaneity. It is a breeding ground for serendipitous teaching and learning moments that can include *any* student at *any* language level at *any* time in the school year. Remember, diversity is not the problem, standardization is, yet we do not have to be victims in the system.

Taking Action Within Standardization

Despite outside influences that can impact curriculum and instruction, there is a call to take action in the ELA classroom. Gilbert (2014) calls upon secondary ELA teachers to engage in subterfuge, a cunning reinterpretation of the "rules" in order to privilege student learning above all else. This means negotiating and questioning policies that do not benefit our students. For adolescent ELs, this entails questioning policies that discourage their midyear entrance in school when it is inconvenient because of testing accountability. Subterfuge means bringing in literature that will be relevant and affirming to our students while questioning curriculum that does not account for their bilingual identities. Campano (2007) reminds us to remember why we are in the classroom and to whom we are accountable. Surely, our accountability and fidelity should be to the unique students we serve, who are perhaps the driving force of why we do what we do. We must remember our students and consider them over fidelity to a program, a curriculum, a textbook, or even other stakeholders.

This will require teachers to take adaptive action—that is, to purposefully consider how to work within the system: to consider what changes you can make, rather than concentrating on what you cannot change (Patterson, Holladay, & Eoyang, 2013). We need to focus on what our core beliefs are for teaching the language arts to English learners—what we believe to be nonnegotiable. Then, we need to understand the constraints around us and what we can do to remove or minimize those restraints.

Patterson and colleagues (2013) explain that adaptive action requires thinking about the different drivers within a system, determining which ones we can change. Often, one change that might seem insignificant can lead to another, creating a greater impact. One significant change that some teachers and I have made is in the curriculum by adding literature that is at the appropriate language level for students and is interesting to them, including adolescent novels, picture books, short stories, and poetry. This addition has resulted in more engaged reading and better student writing products in response to that reading, which we can share with administrators and other teachers, paving the way for more change. Strategies for transformation like this one begin with one purposeful and thoughtful change that puts students first. Perhaps by taking this stance, you will realize there is actually more you can change than you previously assumed.

FIVE SIMPLE RULES FOR LITERACY AND LANGUAGE LEARNING

There are surely many obstacles within the system that get in the way of the high expectations we have for our English learners, yet we can take adaptive action by purposefully considering the patterns that have emerged in our classroom that are a result, at least in part, of the environment we have established. One pattern is for students to bring a notebook to class every day and have it out on their desks when the bells rings, expecting to write. A different pattern would be for students to show up without a writing utensil or notebook and talk among themselves or play on their phones for minutes after the bell rings. Students could regularly place books in their backpacks, knowing you expect them to read at home, or, they might never take a book home, leaving your classroom library untouched. The latter could occur because teachers have never expected them to read at home or because it is just too difficult for students to remember all the regulations in checking out a book from your class. Over time, these patterns can become norms, principles, or guidelines that may either be explicit or unspoken (Patterson et al., 2013). Complexity researchers sometimes call these **"simple rules"**—patterns in our behavior that emerge from the interactions of people in the system and that tend to influence subsequent practices, attitudes, and discourse within the system (Tytel & Holladay, 2011). They are not rules in the sense of laws imposed from above or classroom rules that focus on compliant behavior. They are more like the conventions of grammar—patterns in the ways we use language become rules over time. We agree to follow these rules because they are functional and help build coherence in the system. They are similar to what might be more commonly referred to as classroom routines (Garrett, 2014), yet they differ in how they become more deeply ingrained in the system of our classroom.

For example, I once entered an ESL class and asked students to take out their writing journals, which might be referred to as a routine. When they did not have writing journals or notebooks, I asked them to take out any kind of paper and a writing utensil. Yet, after most students still could not produce those items, I realized that was a pattern of behavior that was governed by an unspoken simple rule that the students and teacher were blindly following: "We do not write in our ESL class." I have also entered an ESL class where students immediately took out a notebook and pencil and looked to the screen to begin their warm-up writing activity. This routine was also guided by an unstated simple rule: "We write to learn and understand our own ideas every day." Although this teacher excellently brought this rule into her classroom without having to state it, stating these rules to help us evaluate patterns in the ways we interact with one another in the classroom can be very effective.

Nonetheless, whether we acknowledge them or not, these simple rules set conditions to influence the patterns in complex systems—such as the ways teachers and students interact with one another (Wickstrom et al., 2011). I have seen patterns that do not support relevant, engaging, or affirming literacy instruction for ELs, such as students just hanging out through their entire ESL block in the name of "needing a break" or being dragged through a text that is far beyond their reading level with no support for the sake of "covering the curriculum." These alarming patterns emerge out of the current educational system and can be seen even in the most caring and competent teachers' classrooms. These undesirable patterns can be referred to as "signal fires" (Tytel & Holladay, 2011) because they point out undesirable behavior that results from unhealthy patterns within the system. These signal fires illustrate the need to seek ways to weaken the patterns that emerge from a system built on testing, grading, accountability, and even a tender heart that feels sorry for ELs. One way to weaken those patterns is to develop a set of shared simple rules that set conditions for patterns that will support relevant, engaging, and affirming literacy in our classrooms.

Because I noticed these signal fires in classrooms I was participating in, I created simple rules for my literacy teaching for a summer literacy institute that other teachers have adopted or modified to fit their classrooms (Stewart, 2016). These rules grew from my concerns that existing classroom routines separated the teacher from the students. I wanted to explicitly emphasize that students and teachers should be doing the same things, continually engaged together as a community of literacy and language learners. Following is each rule that governs my interactions with students in the literacy learning environment. The central focus of these rules is modeling, as I show students the actions and attitudes I want members of our learning community to adopt.

Simple Rule #1: I Learn, You Learn

Before I am ever a teacher, I must always be a learner. Students must see me as a learner, engaged in discovery, if they are to become learners as well. There is so much out there for me to learn, especially from a group of diverse students and my learning process needs to be transparent as I learn *with* them and *from* them. I'm certainly not a "sage on a stage" or even a "guide on the side" (King, 1993). I'm right there with them, a fellow learner, engaged in the same process.

Teaching ELs nurtures this idea because I always have much to learn from my students—including their cultures, experiences, and even names. They see me learn their languages as well, even if it is just a few words that I stumble over each time. As we begin a new unit, I pose questions that I do not have an answer to and eagerly engage in discovery with them to explore potential responses. I should be the lead learner in the classroom, modeling how I'm using literacy and language to gain knowledge.

Simple Rule #2: I Teach, You Teach

I regularly tell students that they need to teach me and others about what they know, especially their lived experiences. This is why I purposefully include literature, videos, and photographs that reflect their languages, cultures, countries, experiences, and culturally embedded knowledge. This positions them as teachers so I am not the only person teaching the class. They can follow the example I have set to teach me and others through literacy, their speaking, writing, and other forms of communication, creating an authentic environment for English language acquisition to occur. Furthermore, as I teach them English, I want them to explain to me various parts of their language. As they do this, they nurture an awareness of the similarities and differences between English and their language and realize that I am a language learner, too.

It is essential for everyone in the classroom to view themselves as a teacher because everyone is a crucial part of our community—thus, we cannot go as far or discover as much without everyone's unique perspective. Everyone has a voice, not just the official teacher, and with that voice comes the responsibility of fully participating in our learning community. When everyone is a teacher, no one can sit in the back and check out—all minds are needed to provide unique contributions.

Simple Rule #3: I Read, You Read

My expectation that students read regularly at school and at home must first be modeled in my life. They need to know "the Miss" is a reader. I read texts that I think the students I'm presently working with might like and I talk about what I've read with them, providing my response to a particular text. Because I have read most of the literature I bring for the students to choose from for independent reading, I can make good recommendations based on the students' interests and language level. During class, when students are reading independently, I am as well. It's important for teachers to forego the need to check email or complete other tasks and allow the students to see them engaged in reading. Sometimes I choose a book in my L2, Spanish, to read and discuss how difficult starting a book in my L2 can be, yet how once I get into the story, I forget I'm even reading in my second language.

This is why I think it's important for us not to persistently rely on teaching through (or fighting through) the same novels each year if we are not strictly mandated to do it. We should constantly be reading and discovering new titles to share with our students each unit, deciding if a whole-class model is even appropriate for our thematic discovery. If we are excited about reading and sharing new stories with our students, then that will affect their view of reading as well.

Simple Rule #4: I Write, You Write

There is nothing teachers should suggest their students write that they will not write themselves. As suggested by classroom writing expert Donald Graves (1983) over 20 years ago, when students write in their writing journals, I do, too, usually sitting beside them. Although this is so simple, it is truly powerful and allows me to enter into a closer relationship with my students. We write together, revise together, and edit final copies of our writing together: R.E.A.L. teachers write personal narratives, biographical poetry, and persuasive essays in responses to literature with their students, sometimes publishing them together in one collection. When students write about themselves and I write about my own life, our relationship strengthens as we share this with one another.

In one class, we wrote about difficult times in our lives in response to a character's situation in a short story we read together. Because some of us shared our journal writing, the students learned about how I had recently lost my grandmother. Then, as they shared their writing, I learned about some of the difficult good-byes they had said to loved ones. Through our writing, we shared our grief and celebrated the people who had made significant impacts in our lives.

Simple Rule #5: I Care About You, You Care About Others (and Maybe Me, Too!)

I read *Number the Stars* (Lowry, 1989) in the 4th grade and it changed my life. Reading that short novel about the Holocaust helped me learn to care about others, even those who are a different religion, nationality, age, or who live in another part of the world. Because I learned to care about people through literacy, I want my students to do so as well. By reading about others and hearing the stories of their classmates, I hope that they will become more caring. As I genuinely inquire about students' language, culture, country, and life experiences, I want them to know that I care about them as individuals and I also expect that they begin to care about one another as they discover how they are alike and different.

Perhaps this is best illustrated through a classroom anecdote with Camille, one of the most interesting students I have taught. Seventeen years old and in her fifth year in U.S. schools, she showed virtually no progress on the assessments used to measure her English development. She rarely spoke, certainly not to other students, and although they had classes with her, they did not know her. After she completed an essay about her life, using her English to explain the trauma she experienced before coming to the United States, she whispered to me once everyone left class one day that she could not read her writing out loud like the other students were doing because she would cry too much. I then asked her if she would rather not share her essay in the class anthology we were publishing, but she quickly shook her head and stated, in a slightly more audible voice, that she wanted all of her classmates and teachers to read about her life and to know her. (Figure 2.1 shows Camille's essay.) Once others had read her writing and began to understand the constant upheaval of the first 11 years of her life as she lived in many different countries, they understood a little more why she did not talk or participate much in class. Her resilient and close extended family was her only constant, so she became accustomed to just speaking to them, basically shutting down at school. After they read her essay, I noticed the other students begin to reach out to her a little more, sitting next to her, asking her questions, and acknowledging her in class.

Finally, I hope that by engaging in these literacy experiences together, students might even begin to care about me. They show their care in different ways. Some will write me notes, send me emails, or simply ask me how I am doing. After a summer class, one student sent me a text message wishing me a safe drive home, even telling me she loved me. Another student might just barely catch my eye and give a quick nod not to be seen by others, making sure I see him put that book in his backpack before he goes home for the weekend and sending the message that he just might read a little. Either way, our students are capable of truly caring about us as teachers. When we are bold enough to open our hearts, they might follow and possibly give us far more than we could ever give them.

These are my five simple rules that I have used to take adaptive action within a system that does not seem to always share my same values, such as building relationships, putting the students' best interest first, and expecting transformative biliteracy and language learning. They have helped me set the conditions for the patterns I want to see—authentic reading and writing

Figure 2.1. Camille's Essay

Congo

I was born in the Congo. The Congo has abundant wildlife and plants. Many people have families and the government said no people could go to school. Life is so important to many people and my parents said we had to move from our country because the government said we could not have freedom.

Zambia

In Zambia it was so different. There were many people there who did not have freedom in their countries. My father had good kids and a good wife. The government wanted to kill my father. He had to pay them money to keep our house. When my sister, Miriam, was born, the government told my mother and father that they wanted to kill her. They wanted to kill many people and damaged many homes so about 30 percent of the people moved to another country.

Tanzania

In Tanzania the government said the children had to go to school to learn Swahili or English. The government told my father he had to give them one of his daughters to be a soldier's wife but he said no because they would kill her. Then we moved to Mozambique.

Mozambique

The government said that we had to speak one language because they would kill the people who spoke my language, Kirundi. My father said we had to move to another country. My parents told us that the government killed my brother and my sister.

South Africa

In South Africa many people died because they did not have a job to make money. In my house we did not have water so we went to the forest to fetch water. The government wanted my father to go to the forest because they wanted an animal to kill him. The government killed my big brother. They also almost killed my mother and little sister when they tried to see my big brother.

Zomba

In Zomba we saw more people die in the forest. The government killed women and children.

Zimbabwe

In Zimbabwe, my family had a big problem. My sister's husband died. People came to the church to kill him. There were many Congolese workers in Zimbabwe. I went to school in Zimbabwe.

America

I was 11 years old when I moved here.

in the classroom, teacher and students learning from one another, everyone fully participating and sharing their perspectives, and all learners (teacher included) gaining empathy and understanding as we learn together in community. These rules place responsibility on me, but they also place responsibility on my students to respond to the example I hope to set.

Other English teachers have used these simple rules, even discussing them with their students. They might also work well for you, but you can develop your own simple rules to fit your unique situation. Whatever your simple rules are, I encourage you to share them with your students or create them together as a class to give everyone a voice in the kind of literacy learning environment you want to have.

ACTION TIME

- Name the goals you want for your ELs. Tell them about these goals (for example: become fully bilingual and biliterate; give a political speech in two languages; develop a bilingual résumé; graduate high school; pursue postsecondary education; obtain a graduate degree).

- Institutionalize the high expectations you have for your students through implementing the Seal of Biliteracy in your school. Go to the Seal of Biliteracy's website (www.sealofbiliteracy.org) and determine if this exists in your state and how you can support it at your own school.

- Read books that your students might find interesting so you can be at the ready to recommend appropriate literature or talk to them about what they are reading.

- Determine which parts of the educational system create obstacles to delivering relevant, engaging, or affirming literacy instruction. Write down one way you could take action within the system.

- Read when your students read and write when they write, despite the increasing number of emails to return or papers to grade. Share your writing with them, even if it makes you vulnerable.

- Use my simple rules or develop your own with your students. Post them on the wall of your classroom and talk about them regularly, asking students how you are doing as a class to stick to your rules. Use them to guide your curriculum, instruction, and relationship with students.

- Read more about adaptive action and simple rules in Patterson, Holladay, and Eoyang's (2013) book, *Radical Rules for Schools: Adaptive Action for Complex Change*.

CHAPTER 3

Read in a
Literature-Rich Classroom

Kelly is a very experienced ELA and ESL teacher who studied second language acquisition in graduate school and has excellent rapport with students. When I entered her English I class for students who were primarily considered long-term ELs, she told me, "It might be rough." She was right. We gave the students a written survey about what they might want to read, and most of them responded that they didn't want to read about anything because they did not like reading at all. I appreciated their honesty, realizing that the 2 months I had to spend with them at the end of the year might be challenging. Kelly and I were up for it, though, and we added dozens of carefully selected books that we thought might engage the students to the classroom library where students could select literature to use for a project they were completing about immigration—a topic students had expressed interest in perhaps because it affected all of their lives in several ways. These books included various genres, reading levels, and even languages, creating a literature-rich classroom that we hoped would facilitate their interactions with texts. At the end of those 2 months, I overheard students Jessica and Isabel talking in class after having taken their state's high-stakes tests that week. They said they were so bored once they finished and wished they had had the novel they had been reading independently in class, *Strange Parents* (Castilla, 2009), to read after finishing. Though they hadn't yet become lifelong readers, for these students who had initially seemed turned off to literature, this was a step in the right direction—they wanted to finish the novel they had selected in class to read.

We often think of early childhood classrooms as places full of different kinds of literature with special reading spaces for the children to enjoy. Yet, adolescents—particularly those who are developing literacy, second language, and bilingual skills—need a literature-rich classroom as well. I want to walk into classrooms where I can see shelves or bins full of books of different genres, levels of complexity, and languages. I want to see a diverse grouping of books within a theme on display and observe student responses to reading about this theme on the walls.

READING WITHIN A THEME

I begin planning for R.E.A.L. instruction by ensuring that there is a vast and diverse amount of literature available for reading in class and at home within a determined theme. Thematic instruction is often recommended for young language learners (Freeman & Freeman, 2006) in order to show them connections across disciplines to maximize content and language learning. **Inquiry-based learning** in the secondary ELA class is also a recommended practice to help students make real-life connections through their learning by deeply exploring a topic (or theme) through posing questions and research-ing answers or solutions (Beach et al., 2016); thus, the adolescent ELs we teach can especially benefit from these practices. Focusing reading around a central idea also maximizes students' vocabulary learning, which is crucial because second language acquisition takes time (Cummins, 1979). English learners need multiple exposures to words to make them part of their **recep-tive vocabulary** (what they can understand through reading or listening) and their **productive vocabulary** (what they can produce through speaking or writing) (Baker, 2011). It is important that we facilitate this language growth because secondary ELs face the challenge of attending multiple class-es, all while learning language and content that usually do not present obvi-ous connections.

If we want students to acquire as much language as possible in the ELA or ESL classroom, we need to place their learning in context each day. We can facilitate their language acquisition by learning within a theme, providing students with several contextually embedded encounters with thematically or-ganized vocabulary and ideas which can be displayed on a word wall, a visual of keywords pertaining to the category being studied (Cloud et al., 2010). Words can be grouped into other categories that might be parts of speech (verbs, nouns, adjectives, adverbs) or by their relationship to the theme (in a World War II unit, for example, words can be grouped by the different events happening around the world). Thematic word walls containing key language within the theme can be utilized as learners continually encounter this vocab-ulary through input (reading and listening) and are expected to produce these words through their output (writing and speaking). Students will become accustomed to looking at the visuals on the classroom wall and the teacher can point to different words or groups of words when mentioning them to fur-ther facilitate students' comprehension. Because the academic vocabulary we are teaching needs to be context-embedded (Freeman, Freeman, & Mercuri, 2002; Gibbons, 2009), students need to read these words in multiple formats, hear them used within context, have opportunities to say them while talking with partners or small groups, and finally, be able to use them effectively in written language. When ELs are fully immersed in an engaging theme, their language and vocabulary development can flourish.

The key in choosing an appropriate theme is to know your students, their interests, lived experiences, and language levels. In order to make effective decisions that are student-centered, we need to ask:

- Is the theme *relevant* to your unique group of students?
- Is the theme *engaging* to students' interests?
- Does the theme lend itself to cultural and language *affirming* instruction?
- Can students explore multiple kinds of *literacy* through the theme while using their current literacy practices as assets to instruction? (For example, Will they have multiple opportunities to engage in reading various literature that is accessible to them? Will they be able to respond through various forms of speaking, writing, or the arts?)

In order to capture students' interest, we need to ensure that we can make the theme relevant to their lives—to give them a reason why we are investigating a particular topic (such as the right to vote) or question (such as, What is the legacy of Cesar Chavez and Dolores Huerta and how can we continue their work?). We also need to be mindful to engage students with one another as we introduce the theme in order to garner as much enthusiasm as possible for the learning that will occur. Furthermore, we should ask ourselves if we are affirming students (their cultures, languages, personal histories, and present situations) through the theme and what opportunities they will have for literacy development through the exploration.

Some themes might entail multiple texts or activities that will take extended amounts of time such as a 9-week grading cycle. Shorter units, such as 2 weeks, might be needed to fill a window between two longer units, or you simply might not have enough literature to extend it further. Regardless of the length of the unit, ELs can greatly benefit from language acquisition and motivation provided by teaching through thematic instruction in the ESL or ELA classroom. This instruction would be even more beneficial if you could recruit teachers in other content areas, such as social studies or the arts, to extend the learning even more by incorporating the same theme in their classrooms. (See Table 3.1 for thematic unit ideas and see the Appendices for a detailed example of the literature used in a short unit on Rosa Parks and a longer-term unit on World War II.)

In order to develop thematic instruction, you will need a large amount of literature—ideally 20 or more texts—that can be used in different ways, so not every student will read every text. A place to start might be Colorín Colorado's book lists (http://www.colorincolorado.org/books-authors/books-kids), which include diverse and multilingual children's and adolescent books categorized under themes. However, only use this as a starting place because you can find further books within a theme by using the resources on the

Table 3.1. Thematic Unit Ideas

Short-Term Themes (2–4 weeks)	Long-Term Themes (5–10 weeks)
Author study (e.g., Alma Flor Ada, Pam Muñoz Ryan, Naomi Shihab Nye)	Civil rights (study in July to remember the signing of the Civil Rights Act of 1964 or in February in conjunction with Black History Month)
Cesar Chavez (Cesar Chavez Day is celebrated March 31 to remember his birth)	War and peace (study in conjunction with Veterans Day in November or Memorial Day in May)
Martin Luther King (MLK Day is in January)	Democracy (coordinate with election day, which is in November in the United States)
Family relationships (Grandparents Day is in September, Mother's Day is in May, Father's Day is in June, and Siblings Day is in April)	The refugee experience (World Refugee Day is in June)
Fitting in and standing out (October is National Bullying Awareness Month and a good time to discuss issues of acceptance crucial for adolescents)	Immigration (the United Nations calls attention to migration on International Migrants Day in December)
Specific regions (e.g., Middle East) or countries (The website kidworldcitizen.org contains information on specific countries that can be used in the classroom in conjunction with a particular holiday or event)	Natural resources and sustainability (the United Nations names March 22 World Water Day each year to bring awareness to the water crisis affecting 1.8 billion people)
The right to vote (August 26 is Women's Equality Day to commemorate women receiving the right to vote in the United States)	Overcoming difficulties (World Day to Overcome Extreme Poverty is in October)
How we use language (International Mother Language Day is celebrated in February)	Women who changed the world (March is Women's History Month)
Where I'm from and who I am (Excellent for the beginning of the school year)	Heritage, lineage, and ancestors (use anytime to learn about students)

Worlds of Words website (www.wowlit.org) and journals such as *The Dragon Lode* (http://www.clrsig.org/the_dragon_lode.php), or *The ALAN Review* (http://scholar.lib.vt.edu/ejournals/ALAN/index.html). Other resources to find sufficient literature for the theme are children's and adolescent book awards listed below, which can be found on the Internet:

- Notable Books for a Global Society
- Skipping Stones Honor Award
- Pura Belpré Award
- Coretta Scott King Book Award
- Ezra Jack Keats Book Award
- Tomás Rivera Book Award
- Asian/Pacific American Award for Literature
- American Indian Youth Literature Award
- Young Adult Library Media Services Book Awards
- Américas Award
- IBBY Honour List

In addition to books, students can also read journalistic articles online. Some online sources for articles, such as News ELA (https://newsela.com/) or the Smithsonian's Tween Tribune (http://tweentribune.com/), allow you to choose the difficulty of the text in English, so you can easily adjust for learners at different levels. I really like Wonderopolis (http://wondero-polis.org/) for nonfiction articles because throughout the text, many words are highlighted and when you scroll over them, a definition appears. This annotated text provides scaffolding for language learners when they need it. DogoNews (https://www.dogonews.com/) also provides articles with words that link to a dictionary definition, which can be useful for vocabulary development and comprehension.

METHODS FOR CLASSROOM READING

Sparking students' interest through thematic inquiry and providing a large amount of engaging, accessible, and diverse literature will further their reading at school and at home. There are various ways students can engage in reading within a theme that can add excitement for classroom reading. The reading methods that can best promote literacy gains for English learners are the teacher **read-aloud, shared reading, guided reading, close reading,** and **independent reading** (Freeman & Freeman, 2006) which are discussed in more detail later. The value of some of the reading methods we might have experienced growing up, such as round-robin reading or popcorn reading, are not supported by research and often cause more damage than good (Optiz & Rasinki, 1998), particularly for students learning English. If you are lucky enough not to have experienced these, round-robin reading is when students take ordered turns reading a text out loud, and popcorn reading is when the teacher randomly calls on someone to read aloud part of a text and then randomly calls another student. Optiz and Rasinki (1998) explain that these methods do not promote comprehension, a key factor for students acquiring a second language. Comprehension is sacrificed because round-robin and popcorn reading often incite anxiety and/or embarrassment to read out loud, which can be heightened for students who are still improving their pronunciation or who have accents that differ from those of their non-EL classmates. These practices also model an inaccurate view of reading because we are rarely called upon to read out loud in our daily lives. Researchers (Optiz & Rasinki, 1998) note that these methods take valuable classroom time away from students who could be engaging with texts in more productive ways.

I often hear students themselves tell me how much they dislike round-robin reading and, in their opinion, they do not learn very much from this method. This is an excerpt of an interview I had with Nathan, an EL in his second year in the United States:

> *Mandy:* How do you read in most of your classes?
> *Nathan:* We have a lot of reading, like each person reads a chapter. At first, I was nervous and I didn't like it, but I got used to it.
> *Mandy:* Do you understand when you read that way in class?
> *Nathan:* Not really. When we are reading some people go fast.
> *Mandy:* So it's hard to follow along?
> *Nathan:* Yes.
> *Mandy:* If you were in charge, how would you do it?
> *Nathan:* I would have the teacher read normal so we can follow along.

Nathan's personal experience reflects research indicating that we forego comprehension with round-robin reading. I highly discourage these ineffective antiquated reading methods; however, there are other practices we can use to add variety to the way we read in R.E.A.L. instruction. Of course, when you ask teachers for their definitions of different reading methods, you will probably get a variety of answers depending on the age of their students or their experience with ELs. In the next section, I do not presume to give the ultimate definition of these reading methods, but instead define generally what I mean by each term in relation to a secondary classroom with students learning English.

Read-Alouds

For the purpose of this book, read-alouds are when the teacher reads the text out loud to the class while the students listen but cannot see the written words. I sometimes use this method for sharing thought-provoking picture books with students as we discuss the visuals and text during the reading in an interactive style. Read-alouds are very beneficial for literacy instruction, even for older learners (Albright & Ariail, 2005; Layne, 2015), yet a student's ability to make meaning from listening to the text, without seeing the words, can differ greatly depending on his or her ability to understand the reader. As a result, when I engage in read-alouds with adolescent ELs at the beginning or intermediate levels of language acquisition, I often see students straining to see the words because they want to follow along or they may ask for a copy of the text. In order to improve listening comprehension in multileveled classes, you can read aloud a short book, poem, or passage for students who can understand without the text, but provide a copy of your read-aloud to others who need more support for comprehension. However, if you find your students regularly arguing over who gets your second copy of the text while you read, you might consider using shared reading more often.

Shared Reading

Shared reading is the term I use to define the practice of the teacher reading aloud fluently from a text while students follow along in their individual copies or by looking at a screen where the text is visibly projected. Adolescent ELs convey to me that they enjoy shared reading with their teachers; for example, Nathan tells me, "The best thing the teacher does to help me learn English is read from a book for me to hear. Then, I look at the words in my own book. That helps me." Repeatedly, students at all levels of English proficiency express that their favorite classroom activity is when their teacher reads them an engaging text, pausing for clarification and response, while they follow along with their own copy. They prefer hearing and seeing the text simultaneously, benefitting from the teacher's reading fluency and maybe even character voices, pauses, and voice inflections, which help students make meaning from the text. Hearing and seeing the printed word simultaneously is a sweet spot of second language acquisition; students have more cues to help them comprehend—even more so with visuals. Although shared reading is expensive because of the need to purchase class sets of reading materials, the language benefits and student enjoyment make it worthwhile. Shared reading is also beneficial for continual interaction among the students and for building a classroom community as you engage with a text together (Boyles, 2014).

Guided Reading

You will also need class or small group sets of texts to engage students in guided reading as students' English proficiency improves. Although guided reading has many definitions, most basically, it is small-group instruction where there is a specific purpose or strategy that the teacher wants to impart during the reading (Burkins & Croft, 2010). I think it is usually more beneficial for adolescent ELs to read silently rather than taking turns to read the text out loud. Sometimes, I use the idea of guided reading with the entire class when separating into small groups is not feasible. There are various ways you can structure guided reading, but at the secondary level, it often entails the students reading a short passage of a text silently and independently with specific instructions from the teacher such as the following:

- Look for words that describe how the character feels.
- Underline the adjectives the author uses to describe the atmosphere in the room.
- As you read this page, think about what the author is trying to make you feel.
- Use the context to understand words you do not recognize in the poem.
- What is the difference between what the character thinks and what he does in Chapter 2?
- Find all of the vocabulary related to our theme in this section.
- What strong words are used in the article that illuminate the writer's view on this issue?

After students have read the short passage independently, the small group or class clarifies the meaning collectively and discusses what they were directed to look for while reading. Although I have used guided reading with many groups of ELs, they usually ask me to go back and read the passage out loud to them after they read it silently by themselves—shared reading. (If I only had a dime for every time I've heard "Now you read it, Miss!") Consequently, if I am reading a novel with a class or small group, I might use a combination of shared and guided reading to change up our interactions with the text.

Close Reading

Close reading is a form of reading that is receiving more attention and can be used in a shared or guided reading context (Boyles, 2014). In close reading, the teacher might select a short text that is at the students' instructional level—that is, a text that is a little too difficult for students to understand without scaffolding—and then attempt to bring the text and the reader close together through intense focus (Beers & Probst, 2013). For example, a teacher might want to introduce a class of ELs to the first page of the novel written in verse *The Crossover* (Alexander, 2014). She can read the page out loud while students follow along in their own copies, then they can discuss the word choice as well as the visual images with this text while reviewing parts of speech and clarifying slang words like *crunking*. The same text might be used for 15 minutes a day for an entire week because there is much to discuss. It is best to have copies for the students to write on so they can annotate their reading each day. Each time the teacher reads the poem or text excerpt aloud, she helps the students dig deeper, discerning the author's meaning and thinking about what he wants readers to feel. Be careful not to engage in close reading for too long with a piece of literature, or your ELs will be less likely to have meaningful engagements with literature or learn to love reading (Gallagher, 2009). For your ELs, think of close reading as broccoli. Yes, it's good for you, but who wants to eat it all day?

Independent Reading

Finally, independent reading is extremely important for adolescent English learners of all language levels—yes, even brand-new beginners. Although students should be encouraged to read anything they want independently, it's good to provide options for independent reading within themes that the class is exploring together, because through investigating a theme, students might grow particularly interested in a topic and want to delve into it more deeply by themselves. If you want to cover a topic broadly but do not have time to read everything you would like together as a class, you can also have students choose literature to read independently for a sharing activity. For example, students can read various picture books about the civil rights movement and then share their learning in groups to help everyone understand different facets of this tumultuous and complex time period. Regardless of how you choose to structure independent reading, setting up a classroom library around a theme with books on display will be key in engaging students in reading in school and at home. At school, this might occur in what is commonly referred to as sustained silent reading (SSR) or D.E.A.R. time (drop everything and read), which is very beneficial because your classroom might be the quietest and most comfortable place students have to read silently and develop recreational reading habits. Yet teachers need to ensure that SSR is truly a time for students to read what they enjoy, find interesting, and comprehend (Gallagher, 2009), and for ELs that might mean reading in their L1 some or even most of the time. I strive to follow my Simple Rule #3 during SSR as well and read my book of choice while the students read, instead of tutoring, grading, or completing other tasks.

It's equally important to expect and facilitate students' reading at home by sending books home from the school or your classroom library just as Marie and I initiated the "spring to summer" campaign by requiring students to have a self-selected book in their backpack when they left. My conversations with ELs tell me that these students are often intimidated to check out books from the school library or are unaware of the selection available. I think it is best to build your own classroom library and keep the books visible to students at all times—not shut away in a closet and theoretically locked away because of difficult borrowing procedures. In one class, I was helping students choose books from the teacher's selection when she was gone, but even I was intimidated by the complicated checkout system that basically made them promise their first-born child if they didn't return a book. Therefore, I brought my own books for them to borrow and, honestly, some of those books never came back. In fact, many of my books are out there in the possession of these high schoolers, but I'm much more concerned with getting a reader back, a student who returns over the weekend telling me about what he read and asking for another book, than getting the actual books themselves back. My solution is, whenever possible, to buy used and consider whatever does not come back a donation to creating a better world for us all to live in. (You're welcome!)

Certainly, the various ways we structure classroom reading (read-alouds, shared reading, SSR, and so forth) are nuanced topics that are the focus of entire resource books written by knowledgeable professionals (e.g., Beers & Probst, 2013; Burkins & Croft, 2010; Galda & Graves, 2007; Layne, 2015). Although I certainly encourage you to investigate these resources to determine a regular classroom reading plan, the main point in R.E.A.L. instruction is that you understand why you are facilitating students' engagement with text in a certain way (understand the theory and research that motivate your decisions) and remember that most of this reading is occurring in students' second language. As you listen to other rock star teachers' ideas, attend conferences, or read professional development materials, always consider if the rock star/author/speaker has ELs as their main focus, because sometimes what might be an incredible idea for adolescents in their L1 might not be the best method for a student engaging in second language acquisition. Knowing the many options available, think about how you would want to engage with a text if you were reading in a language you were acquiring.

Considering the different benefits of various methods of reading for ELs can help you know how to structure your weekly class meetings. When I'm teaching, I commit to reading aloud to students every day, even if it is only briefly, and I often display the text for students who can benefit from more support. I rely heavily on shared reading, sprinkled with guided, close, and independent reading during class time throughout the week. During independent reading, I make sure the students see me read and I especially want them to see me read in my second language, Spanish, to know that I am walking in their shoes as a language learner. Lastly, I expect much independent reading from students outside of class and do everything I can to facilitate this—talking to students about their schedules, brainstorming times they could read, and regularly discussing what they would like to read and in what language.

Although the language levels of your students might vary, ELs need a healthy diet of all these research-based components of reading in order to acquire language. Modifications are necessary for individual students within each reading method through the amount of support and structure you provide. The literature you choose and its genre, language, and level of complexity will also allow you to make modifications to your classroom's reading routines. The next part of this chapter discusses the various kinds of literature you can include in your literature-rich classroom.

MULTIPLE GENRES

Within each theme, we should use multiple genres of literature with ELs, knowing that each genre has a special component in helping students develop literacy, language, and bilingualism (Freeman & Freeman, 2006). Remember, ELs should be swimming in the vast amount of literature you provide them access to around a theme and for other self-selected reading.

Narratives

Narratives build on students' existing understanding of stories. Students will probably already have an idea of a setting, rising action, climax, and resolution (even if they do not know those terms) through past reading or oral stories in their languages. Reading narratives connects to this prior knowledge and allows students to become familiar with grammatical elements of the English language while learning how language is used in natural ways.

Most important, stories provide a way for students to get lost in their reading by connecting to the characters who might be like them in some way or learning about people who are different. Stories allow students to develop empathy for others as they understand what it is like to be someone else. Andrés told me he loved reading the stories about historical events because they helped him understand the past by learning about people's lives. He learned about the atomic bombs in Japan in his history class but told me he really learned about those events through reading a graphic novel in Spanish about a boy his age who lived through those events, *Pies Descalzos—Barefoot Gen* in the English version (Nakazawa, 1987).

In my experience, narratives—whether they are fiction, historical fiction, or even biographical accounts of someone's life—are what most adolescent ELs love the most. It's through narratives that they beg me, "Miss, keep reading please. We want to know what happens." For students who have never read a book in English or who are turned off to literature in any language, stories can be a tempting invitation into the world of reading.

Because it is an inspiring story, students might enjoy the picture book *Emmanuel's Dream: The True Story of Emmanuel Ofosu Yeboah* (Thompson & Qualls, 2015) within a theme about overcoming difficulties, children who changed the world, or heroes. It could be a great read-aloud or a selection for independent reading. I've read *Esperanza Rising* (Ryan, 2000) as shared reading with a group of beginning to advanced ELs, including long-term ELs, who spoke Vietnamese and Spanish. Fast-paced and based on historical events, the beautiful story can be understood to some degree by most students with appropriate support. One day I overheard (I overhear a lot when students forget that I speak Spanish!) two girls who had seemed uninterested in reading and school in general talk about how much they loved the book. Forgetting I could understand them, they discussed whether the teacher might let them have permission to take the book home for the weekend and keep reading. Students asking permission to keep reading at home! That is the beauty of an engaging narrative—it has the power to turn anyone into a lover of books, even if they would never actually admit it in front of their friends. I also recommend *Esperanza Rising* because it can be purchased both in Spanish and as an annotated edition in English. It would fit into a theme about immigration, the Great Depression, agriculture, or overcoming difficulties.

Poetry and Lyrics

Using fewer words to say more is excellent for students acquiring vocabulary in their second language. Some students feel they need to understand every word they are reading, which is cumbersome in reading narratives. I discourage students from translating every word on a page with a lot of text. However, for these particular students, poetry or song lyrics provide reading for which it is more feasible to translate each unknown word. I make copies of poems for students so, if they want, they can write their language in the margins for any new vocabulary. Reading poetry with ELs can also help them with figurative language, which can be a struggle to comprehend in the L2, yet is a crucial literacy skill that they need to develop.

For ELs in particular, poetry can also be an accessible means of close reading, a critical and deep analysis of the text, focusing on details, patterns, nuanced meanings, words, or phrases while considering the author's intent. Going over every word, sentence structure, and detail of longer passages can be excruciating for students if the passage is beyond their level of comprehensible input. A short poem is often the perfect length to engage ELs in close reading practices.

Although poetry provides adolescent ELs with a smaller amount of text, it can still cover relevant topics that are appropriate for these young adults. Some anthologies put into words students' feelings about their bilingualism and biculturalism, such as *Red Hot Salsa: Bilingual Poems on Being Young and Latino in the United States* (Carlson, 2005), a book suitable for an identity theme. Other poems explain daily life in other parts of the world, such as *19 Varieties of Gazelle: Poems of the Middle East* (Nye, 2002) or *The Tree Is Older Than You Are* (Nye, 1995), which can be used when learning about various regions/countries—in this case, the Middle East and Mexico, respectively. Poetry can also cover very mature topics that are engaging for adolescents, such as *A Wreath for Emmett Till* (Nelson, 2005), which recounts the true story of an adolescent boy who was lynched and killed in the United States in 1955, helping students explore the horrible consequences of racism, particularly when you pair this book with the rich poetry and illustrations from *Freedom over Me: Eleven Slaves, Their Lives and Dreams Brought to Life* (Bryan, 2016). When you use this literature in the classroom, students will know they are learning about mature topics and engaging in rigorous critical thinking even through learning English with accessible texts.

As I mentioned before, reading aloud to students learning English is a very important activity that I believe should be accomplished regularly for its multiple benefits (Layne, 2015). Students need to hear you read fluently. It sends them the message that you highly value reading in community. However, in short class periods, especially if it's an assembly day, there might be limited time for a read-aloud or shared reading. You might find a short poem to start the class if there is not time for a longer reading in community.

You can pledge to read a poem every Friday with your students to ensure that they are regularly exposed to poetry. Using a projector or providing copies to engage in shared reading, every student should be able to see the text and engage in listening to you read it, and then read it with you chorally. *The Poetry Friday Anthology for Celebrations: Holiday Poems for the Whole Year in English and Spanish* (Vardell & Wong, 2015) contains poems for every week of the year that are excellent for regular poetry reading that connects to special celebrations and events. The poems in this bilingual anthology, which will fit well into various themes, are written by a diverse group of renowned poets and authors.

Consider using poetry to develop students' listening skills as well by identifying a short poem to read aloud each week from some of the titles mentioned. First, read the poem aloud without allowing students to see the words. Guide them to exercise their listening skills and discuss what they understood with a partner. Then, read the same poem while displaying the words for students and ask them if they now understood more. Each week with a different poem, have students monitor how much more they are able to comprehend without the words. Try bringing in different readers because students often tell me they understand me better than other native-English speakers. (Or maybe, it's because East Texas accents are just easier to understand!) Regardless, helping students track their progress of how much they can understand from the first (no visual) to the second reading (with visual) of a poem with different people reading the text can further their listening skills.

Informational and Expository Text

Although I think themes come alive for students through narratives and poetry, supplemental informational and expository texts can provide students with additional access points to the theme. Informational texts with simple language are useful for helping students develop independent reading skills in their second language—English. I have noticed that adolescent ELs often choose National Geographic Easy Readers to take home to learn more about people within a theme such as Anne Frank or Abraham Lincoln. These leveled readers can also engage students in learning about places, historical events, or facets of nature.

It is important that teachers point out various features of expository text to ELs because these students might not receive direct instruction on reading this genre in the other content-area classes such as social studies and science. A lesson that covers different features of expository text such as titles, headings, subheadings, boldfaced words, and tables can be dry. Yet, when students are further exploring an engaging topic while learning about the expository genre, they might be much more engaged in the same lesson. They will also understand the content (text features) better if it is contextually embedded within a theme. Learning about text features can also develop higher-order thinking if—for example, through reading *Girls Think of Everything: Stories of Ingenious Inventions by Women* (Thimmesh & Sweet, 2000)—students engage in complex discussions about gender stereotypes.

Illustrated expository texts such as *Amelia to Zora: Twenty-Six Women Who Changed the World* (Chin-Lee, Halsey, & Addy, 2005) and *Akira to Zoltán: Twenty-Six Men Who Changed the World* (Chin-Lee, Halsey, & Addy, 2006) contain pages that can be used individually, without the remainder of the book, for various themes or individual student research. Each of these books tells the story of 26 women and men, respectively, who had a great influence on the world—one person for each letter of the alphabet. *Dare to Dream . . . Change the World* (Corcoran, 2012) is a book with which I've been able to use individual pages to introduce different themes. The people included in these texts are from various countries and ELs might already be familiar with some of them.

Wordless Books and Images

Wordless books and images provide ELs with another way to access the theme regardless of their reading level in English. A story told through pictures allows ELs to think about what is happening and use oral or written language to express their thoughts. They can use English or their L1, which provides access to everyone.

Marie, Carlos's teacher who I mentioned in Chapter 2, began a unit centered on the book *Sylvia & Aki* (Conkling, 2011), which occurs during World War II, with a photograph analysis activity. She showed her students evocative pictures illustrating discrimination, segregation, and racism in the United States and Europe. She assigned each group of students a picture and asked them these questions:

1. What is one detail in the photograph?
2. What title can you give it?
3. What is one thing you don't understand?

Students discussed these questions in groups and then individually wrote their responses in a journal. To end the activity, the students shared what their group thought with the class as everyone viewed each photograph (see Figure 3.1 for an example).

The Arrival (Tan, 2006) is a wordless picture book that many teachers have used successfully with ELs for literacy development (Martínez-Roldán & Newcomer, 2011). These beautiful illustrations about the immigrant experiences will provoke many discussions from ELs who have had similar experiences. I used this book with a group of refugee students and was regularly amazed at their insights. Other wordless books with images to facilitate oral and written storytelling are *Flotsam* (Wiesner, 2006), *Zoom* (Banyai, 1995), and *Unspoken: A Story from the Underground Railroad* (Cole, 2012).

Plays

Even though round-robin and popcorn reading are not beneficial to students, you can engage more advanced ELs in oral reading exercises through reader's theater by incorporating plays into your classroom reading (Optiz & Rasinki, 1998). Find scripts for reader's theater online (for example, at http://www.thebestclass.org/rtscripts.html), use engaging plays such as *Novio Boy* (Soto, 2006), or have students create their own scripts. The publisher Benchmark Education has a series of reader's theater scripts from the lives of famous people such as Frederick Douglass. Give students ample time to practice pronunciation, fluency, pauses, and voice inflections, modeling when needed. Do everything you can to ensure their success before allowing them to perform for the class or for a younger grade to build their confidence reading out loud in English. Whereas these works can add variety to your classroom reading, I suggest using them sparingly in order to focus more on the comprehension and language building that adolescent ELs need most in order to be successful on academic measures of achievement. Remember, no one needs to read out loud in order to score high on the SAT, but reader's theater can be a fun way to vary the reading routines in your classroom at certain times.

Student-Created Reference Texts

Throughout a unit of exploration in a theme, students can create their own texts and display them on the walls to refer to throughout the unit. You might ask them to list important characters in a novel that the class is reading, along with character traits. They can also display the plots of the different

Figure 3.1. Photograph Analysis Activity and Student Writing

- The photo is kids.
- The fence is bad.
- I do not understand what they cannot no go to.

books they are reading within the theme to facilitate text-to-text connections. This provides a quick way for students to remember important information to help them in their continual language acquisition and learning within the theme.

In Marie's class, students formed groups to research important topics that were related to the theme of World War II—Pearl Harbor, Japanese internment camps, atomic bombs, Nazis, and the Holocaust. They needed this information to understand the books they would read together as a class and independently. Throughout the unit, Marie, as well as the students, regularly referenced the student-created posters on the wall to recall important information that assisted them in their text comprehension and language acquisition.

Videos as Texts

Multimedia content is an excellent resource to provide students who are learning English with another avenue to make the content comprehensible (Echevarría, Vogt, & Short, 2017), and videos can be considered a text used within a thematic unit. Furthermore, you can facilitate the sharing of complex ideas through video, especially when the closed captioning is turned on so students can see and hear the words in addition to the action on the screen to understand (Parris, Estrada, & Honigsfeld, 2017). Videos about nearly any topic are readily available on Internet sites such as YouTube. Watching short videos can be an interesting way to introduce a topic or provide students with directed listening opportunities.

Videos can also illustrate the importance of what students are learning in the theme; for example, at the beginning of a 2-week unit about Supreme Court Justice Sonia Sotomayor, I showed students a video of her swearing-in ceremony to illustrate the importance of the person they would learn about through literature. Later in the unit, to add variation to a class period of shared reading about poetry from her life, I showed students another video in which she spoke about the same events in her life that we were reading about in the text. In another example, when beginning a unit of study on segregation and reading about Sylvia Mendez, I showed a very short video of Mendez receiving the Medal of Honor from President Obama, whom all the students recognized. This piqued their interest as they began to understand that the 10-year-old girl they would read about over the next few weeks did something very important.

Videos can be used as supplemental texts that provide further opportunities for theme exploration and language acquisition. Short videos might also break up the monotony of long periods of reading and facilitate students' understanding of why what they are learning might be relevant to their lives.

LITERATURE AT VARIOUS READING LEVELS

Secondary teachers, particularly in high schools, often tell me that their school libraries or book rooms do not have much literature with language that is accessible to their beginning or intermediate English learners. These teachers are usually thrilled at the books I bring them, which their students can read successfully. It is important that we get students reading regardless of whether they are reading in English or their first language or if they are reading a text with 10 words or 10,000 words. English learners need to read, and waiting until they have access to the texts traditionally used in secondary ELA classrooms is unacceptable.

Indeed, we need to make sure we provide students with literature at various reading levels to meet them where they are, to push them to the next level, and to engage their first language for further literacy development. For many high school teachers, this means you will need to talk to your librarian about buying books at various levels, purchase books for your own classroom library, or work with your public libraries to check out children's and adolescent books that your high school does not have.

Work diligently to locate texts that students will not view as demeaning—that is, don't make students feel you are treating them like young children just because they are learning English. Approaching a text for its visuals, artistry, word play, or mature themes can assure students that they are learning age-appropriate material.

Illustrated Books with Limited Text

Pictures assist students in making meaning from text. Text that is incomprehensible on its own might become meaningful to students when accompanied with a visual. Fortunately, many illustrated books are presented in artistic formats that can engage older learners. For example, when a book is presented to students as an exemplar in its artistry (such as photography or painting), adolescent ELs will not feel as if they are receiving books written for young children.

Lay Su Aung, an advanced EL student from Myanmar, told me she hated when the teacher just gave them "baby books" to read. I have also noticed that when provided with many books to choose from, some ELs are reluctant to choose an illustrated book, even if they are beginning ELs, because they feel they are too old to read a picture book. If we highlight the artistry in the accompanying illustrations and choose illustrated texts with more mature themes, students can benefit from the language acquisition that can occur through the text that is supported by visual cues.

A Cool Drink of Water (Kerley, 2002) is published by National Geographic with trademark photography showing how people drink and transport water throughout the world. Each page contains only two to 12 words, making this text very accessible to all language learners. Beginners can use the visuals for basic vocabulary acquisition of concrete objects such as *water*, *river*, and *fountains*. More advanced ELs can study the words in the book used to describe water such as *chilled*, *scooped*, *sipped*, and *squeezed*. This book can be in a theme about the shared human experience, cultures around the world, or Earth's natural resources.

English learners can also study picture books by famous illustrators who have developed their own unique style, which is especially effective when the school's art teacher is involved. Through these books, students can study how art portrays meaning while learning within the theme for language acquisition. Brian Pickney is a winner of various awards for his work that illustrates books about African American life such *Boycott Blues: How Rosa Parks Inspired a Nation* (Pinkney & Pinkney, 2008), which might be used in a theme on world changers or the civil rights movement. Duncan Tonatiuh is an author/illustrator from Mexico whose award-winning illustrated books highlight the Latino culture and experience through very distinct illustrations. Read *Pancho Rabbit and the Coyote* (Tonatiuh, 2013) with students in a unit on immigration while teaching the literary mechanism of allegory. Other illustrated books that offer interesting illustrations or cover mature topics that adolescent ELs and I have enjoyed reading together are listed in Table 3.2.

Table 3.2. Additional Illustrated Books with Limited Text Appropriate for Adolescent ELs

Book	Special Features
Brown, M., & Paschkis, J. (2011). *Pablo Neruda: Poet of the people*. New York, NY: Henry Holt and Co.	Illustrator Julie Paschkis has created unique illustrations filled with Spanish and English words, aptly representing the famous Chilean poet, Pablo Neruda.
Yolen, J., & Shannon, D. (1992). *Encounter*. San Diego, CA: Harcourt Brace Jovanovich.	This book helps students think critically about the discovery of the Americas (also available separately in Spanish). It facilitates critical thinking about Columbus Day or Indigenous People's Day. Make sure to note the American Indians in Children's Literature review of this book as you discuss it with students."
Tan, S. (2011). *Lost and found*. New York, NY: Arthur A. Levine Books, an imprint of Scholastic Inc.	This book contains three compelling and thought-provoking short stories that primarily are told through rich visuals accompanied by limited text. These stories are dependent on the author's use of image.
Buitrago J., & Yockteng, R. (2015). *Two white rabbits*. Toronto, Canada: Groundwood Books/ House of Anansi Press.	This timely story portrays the dangerous immigration journey many people from Central America and Mexico take to get to the United States by traveling on foot, rafts, the top of a train, and/or in truck beds. The president of IBBY challenges readers at the end with this question that older students can deeply consider: "What do those of us who have safe comfortable lives owe to people who do not?"
Winter, J. (2010). *Biblioburro: A true story from Colombia*. New York, NY: Beach Lane Books.	The vibrant illustrations and simple text tell a true story from Colombia that can help students learn to highly value all the literature you have provided them. (After reading this book to students, they have lovingly referred to me as the *biblioburro*, the book donkey, because I'm always carrying bags of books with me when I come to their class!)

Graphic Novels

Graphic novels are prime examples of limited text accompanied by illustrations, yet students do not feel they are reading books for young children because this genre often covers mature themes and requires the reader to possess advanced skills such as understanding facial expressions, body language, and other meaning communicated through the visuals (Moeller, 2016). Graphic novels can particularly help English learners develop second language proficiency through the use of visuals that provide the reader with comprehensible input while lessening the anxiety that might come from a book with many unknown words and thereby motivating the student (Cary, 2004). Studies show how graphic novels have been used in classrooms with adolescents to foster academic language with deaf students (Smetana, Odelson, Burns, & Grisham, 2009) as well as to engage ELs with complex topics such as racism (Chun, 2009) and immigration (Boatright, 2010) while assisting them in making connections to their own migration experiences (Danzak, 2011).

Some graphic novels might be considered entertaining, such as the book about teenage vampires that Chen, a newcomer from China, chose to take home for summer reading—*Blue Bloods: The Graphic Novel* (de la Cruz & Venditti, 2013). *American Born Chinese* (Yang, 2006) is a humorous graphic novel that covers the universal notion of fitting in that middle school students read to begin a Graphic Journeys literacy project where they shared their own immigrant experiences (Danzak, 2011). Yet graphic novels can also cover more serious topics such as these two suggestions that tell true stories of grave injustices in the Democratic Republic of Congo and Mexico. *Child Soldier: When Boys and Girls Are Used in War* (Chikwanine & Humphreys, 2015) and *La Lucha: The Story of Lucha Castro and Human Rights in Mexico* (Sack, 2015) can both fit into the themes of justice.

Short Stories

Reading a whole novel in a second language such as English is not linguistically appropriate for some English learners. Just seeing all those words and pages can be overwhelming if they have not yet acquired sufficient vocabulary. Giving students novels that are above their comprehension level may make them feel frustrated, essentially impeding further literacy engagement and language acquisition. Short stories usually have less text and can be completed in a shorter amount of time, making them wonderful additions to thematic units that can provide a bridge to connect students to longer text in English if reading an entire novel is not yet appropriate. For a thematic unit on immigration, try selections from *Papers: Stories by Undocumented Youth* (Galisky & Shine, 2010). These true stories by undocumented teenagers from various countries are of different lengths and text complexity. Some of them are just one page and contain accessible text for a beginning English learner, while others are longer and can provide an engaging challenge for more advanced students, all while exploring a mature and relevant topic. There is also an accompanying video to go along with these relevant stories. "The All-American Slurp" (Namioka, 2003), a single story, and the multiple stories in *First Crossing: Stories About Teen Immigration* (Gallo, 2004) are texts that tackle both difficult and lighthearted situations of the type in which adolescents who have experienced migration might find themselves. The eight short stories in *Santa Claus in Baghdad and Other Stories About Teens in the Arab World* (Marston, 2008) can individually round out themes such as friendship, loyalty, or war. Teachers can collect anthologies that contain many short stories on a wide range of topics from which they can add at least one story within each theme explored in class.

Chapter Books

Reading one's first chapter book, whether it is with a teacher or independently, is a feat many students positively remember. Even 18-year-olds have come to me, proudly showing me the first chapter book they finished in English. Because it is crucial for students to experience sustained reading in English for second language acquisition (Krashen, 2004, 2012), we need to provide students with longer books that contain appropriate text complexity and interesting plots. Some of the books ELs tell me they love the most are chapter books commonly used in the middle grades that tell compelling stories such as *Return to Sender* (Álvarez, 2010) or *A Long Walk to Water* (Park, 2010). Do not hesitate to explore the children's or middle grades section of the library for chapter books that might interest your students even if they are in high school.

It is also important to keep ELs reading in their first language. If they are able to read in their L1, providing them with chapter books within the theme can further their knowledge and allow them to provide a valuable contribution to the class's exploration. Additionally, L1 reading will develop students' literacy skills, which transfer to English (Cummins, 1979) and affirm their language abilities. Chapter books in various languages allow teachers to facilitate students' bilingual development even when they do not speak students' languages. Chapter 6 provides many ideas for first language reading.

ACTION TIME

- Determine a short- or long-term theme that might engage your students. Use the resources provided (World of Words, Colorín Colorado, and award websites) to find 10–20 books that fit your theme. Next, try some of the websites to find an article that fits into the theme. Finally, search YouTube (https://www.youtube.com/) or TedEd (https://ed.ted.com/) to add a video.

- Ask teachers from other content areas if they would like to partner with you in thematic learning. Develop as many cross-disciplinary connections as you can (science, math, history, government, economics, computer science, world languages, sociology, art, music, dance, kinesiology, health, business).

- Diversify your library in regard not only to the content of the books, but also languages, text complexity, and genre. Think about the accessibility students have to your books. Is your borrowing system keeping them from taking books home?
- Read *Wordless Books: So Much to Say!* by Martínez-Alba and Cruzado-Guerreo (2015) for lesson ideas on using wordless picture books for students learning English.

CHAPTER 4

Respond to Texts in a Literacy-Rich Classroom

I am engaging in shared reading using the novel *Inside Out & Back Again* (Lai, 2011) with a small group of 9th- through 12th-grade students who are all refugees and at various stages of L2 acquisition when, at a poignant place in the novel, I pause reading to allow for reflection. Unexpectedly, Khine, a 10th-grade student from Myanmar, tells us he wants to share a connection he has to the text. He begins slowly, searching for the words in English, as we all listen intently. He tells us that like the family in the book who lost one of their own in Vietnam, never making it to America, his brother died in his country. He explains in detail exactly what happened when his baby brother swallowed poisonous liquid and there were no accessible hospitals to save his life, prompting his parents to seek a better life for their other children. Then, organically, all five students in the small group use their emerging English abilities to share about a sibling each of them lost in their home country without any prompting or interjections from me. When they have finished, I sit there with my book, unable to speak, yet oddly knowing I don't need to. These young people are discovering similar life experiences they have that tie them together and, perhaps, sharing with one another is healing. From this point on, I am not the teacher and they are not students—we have become a community.

Indeed, responding to literature together creates community (Beers & Probst, 2013). This particular book generated a bridge from me to my students and connected us in ways I would not know how to facilitate without meaningful stories. Through reader response, your students can share much about themselves, just as you share your life with them. This is the prime way I have developed relationships with English learners in the classroom and it is also how I have witnessed students begin to understand one another as they note similarities in their responses that bridge cultural and linguistic divides.

In addition to developing relationships through reader response, English learners need to regularly respond before, during, and after reading for literacy and language acquisition (Gibbons, 2009). Their responses should be varied, focusing on developing oral language, writing abilities, and critical thinking skills while engaging in creative and artistic endeavors. Students need to routinely respond to communicate their learning, make sense of their reading, develop their literate identities, and become active participants in the classroom literacy community.

Just as there are multiple diverse texts to choose from to read with students, there are also many ways students can respond to their reading. Although there might be particular response activities that seem to work best with your students, I encourage you to push yourself and your students to try to add new reader response activities to your repertoire during each thematic unit of instruction. Variation will keep classroom learning exciting and engage students with new ways of demonstrating their learning as you give them the opportunity to develop different literacies and showcase their strengths. Additionally, I want to emphasize that although I present reading and responding in two distinct chapters in this book, they are activities that should occur together. Thus, students should be responding to a particular text before they begin reading, while they are engaged in the text, and once they are finished. These are often referred to prereading, during-reading, and post-reading activities and could take anywhere from a few minutes to a few days, depending on the complexity and depth of the activity, the students' engagement, and time constraints (Galda & Graves, 2007).

READER RESPONSE THROUGH ORAL LANGUAGE

Adolescent ELs need multiple opportunities to develop their oral English skills (Faltis & Coulter, 2008). Being able to hear and understand as well as say vocabulary that is repeated within a theme is essential in order for students to own the word and retain it in their receptive and productive vocabulary—what they are able to understand from reading and listening as well as what they can produce through writing and speaking (Calderón, 2007). They also need opportunities to discuss literature for personal growth, understanding, and identity development, which can be accomplished through speaking in their L1s in addition to English (Cummins et al., 2005).

Class, Small-Group, and Partner Discussions

Through reading with your students within a planned thematic unit, many interesting questions will surface, which is a great way to further develop your students' critical thinking. You can structure discussions in many different ways to clarify information in a text before moving on, making sure all students understand the plot. Whole-class discussion can be very valuable if you can ensure that all students have equitable access to participate. However, ELs need opportunities to more regularly respond orally to their reading than can be provided in whole-class discussions. Small-group and partner discussions such as turn and talk, allow ELs continual oral practice as they share their ideas and clarify concepts from their reading. One strategy to ensure that everyone has the opportunity to participate in discussion is think, write, pair, share (Herrell, Jordan, & Herrell, 2012), where students are prompted to think about a question from the reading and then write down their thoughts. Next, they pair with another student and each shares his or her response, providing ELs with regular low-stakes opportunities to discuss the text that can be used at any point before, during, or after a reading.

L1 Affinity Groups

I encourage you to attempt to read a book in a language in which you are still developing secondary-level reading skills. Probably, at some point, you will want to make sense of what you are reading in the language you know best. Our students learning English will likely feel the same way when reading literature in a language they are acquiring. Therefore, creating officially sanctioned L1 groups where students can discuss the English text with others in their language can be very useful by capitalizing on collaboration (Ebe & Chapman-Santiago, 2016). Clarifying meaning or discussing opinions about a text in the L1 can even lead to more effective acquisition in the L2, English.

But I know what many of you are thinking: "It's not fair because not all of my students speak Spanish." I agree, and even in Texas, I've rarely been in a secondary English class where all students have someone who speaks their language. Because I speak Spanish and most ELs I work with do as well, I am extra careful to make sure non–Spanish speakers, especially if they do not have another speaker of their language in the class, do not feel left out or unsupported. At the same time, I believe in the benefits of L1 discussion, so I look for solutions to this challenge, rather than removing the opportunity for all students to take advantage of L1 groups.

For example, when I taught 6th grade in a newcomer center, I had one particular class with all Spanish speakers except one Korean speaker named Adam. At strategic times, I arranged the class in small groups and encouraged them to discuss the content I had covered in English with one another in Spanish, yet I partnered Adam with one Spanish-speaking student named Pedro who had received an excellent education in Mexico and had very well-developed literacy and study skills. I spoke to Pedro and asked him if he would be Adam's partner in class, only speaking in English. The partnership was successful and the boys became good friends, enjoying speaking in their emerging English to each other, using L1 dictionaries when needed and even teaching each other a little in their languages. The disadvantage was that the boys did not receive the support of L1 discussion, but I could not provide it for Adam, with no other Korean speakers in the school, and Pedro did not need the content support as much as the other students. The rest of the class could benefit from discussing content in the L1 and I was able to constantly monitor Pedro's comprehension to see when I might need to clarify something for him in Spanish.

In other classes, I've had many Spanish speakers, a couple of Arabic speakers, and then about four other students who all speak different languages. After grouping or partnering students with common L1s, I make a group of students who have to use their only common language, English, to communicate. I am mindful to provide that group extra support with more of my time in helping them in their discussions or activities. I desperately wish I could provide an L1 partner for each student and that I could speak all of their languages; however, that is not reality. Yet, because I highly believe in the benefits of L1 discussion, I often use these viable options so I do not have to take a learning opportunity away from students who can use the L1 with someone in class at strategic times.

Now that I hope I have provided some valid challenges to the fairness argument that often impedes beneficial L1 affinity groups for discussion, I want to provide some examples of how and why I use this strategy, supported by research (Early & Marshall, 2008; García et al., 2017; Ebe & Chapman-Santiago, 2016). Providing students with the opportunity to respond to reading in English using the L1 supports their content learning and literacy development. For example, if a student becomes confused regarding the plot in a text you are reading with the class, he or she might disengage or not comprehend as much as you continue reading. Having the opportunity to discuss the English text at certain intervals in the L1 can make the subsequent section you read with the class more comprehensible, and more comprehensible input will lead to greater second language acquisition (Krashen, 1994).

Generally, second language learners' receptive language will be greater than their productive language (Baker, 2011). That is, ELs might be able to understand (receptive language) more of the reading than they are able to discuss (productive language) in English. Using L1 groups for discussion, even when reading a text in English, allows students to develop their higher-order thinking and advanced literacy skills by analyzing and evaluating the reading in their first languages.

Early and Marshall's (2008) research illustrates how inviting adolescent ELs to work collaboratively in their L1s to make meaning from literary texts read in English facilitates this process. Throughout the reader response project in the class, the teacher would sometimes encourage students to find someone who speaks their language to ensure that they understood the text. When students were interviewed after the project about their L1 use, many stated that they used it to make better sense of complex ideas and to determine the best words in English to express a concept they already understood in their language. The teacher viewed students' L1 as linguistic capital that she could build on in order to nurture their understanding of the literary text.

Teacher Conversations

Students also need to sit down individually or in a small group with their teacher to talk about what they are reading, similar to the same idea in the reading workshop model (Atwell, 1987). I think this is particularly true for English learners, who need multiple opportunities to speak with fluent English speakers. Teachers also need to understand students' engagement with the text in order to guide instruction. If, like me, you love the idea of reading workshop, but always seem to be stretched to find the time to just sit down and have a relaxed conversation with all students about their reading, try joining them for breakfast or lunch. I love it when students want to eat lunch with me to tell me about what they are reading as well as their opinions on the book, connections to the text, and questions they have. These conversations are useful for developing relationships with students and for clarifying information that goes beyond language. A student named Lay Su Aung wanted me to explain American dating norms to her while she was reading the popular book *The Fault in Our Stars* (Green, 2012). She wondered: In the United States, can girls ask boys out on dates? Does a girl have to wait for a boy to ask her first? These are questions that are important for the reader to understand in order to make the most meaning from this text. She also had difficulty keeping all the characters straight in the novel, leading her to proclaim to me: "Too many cute boys!" Understanding the need to know who is who in this particular novel that I had also read, I helped her keep a list of all the characters in the book, their personality, physical appearance, and love interests.

Andrés talked to me over lunch about a book he was reading in Spanish about the atomic bombs in Japan. He asked many questions I did not know the answers to, but that gave us an opportunity to explore the answers together. Through his reading, he also wanted to connect World War II to current times, asking me about current events in the world and if I thought we were heading toward a third world war. Of course, I did not have a concrete answer, but we had some engaging discussion sparked by his reading.

Sara, from Colombia, met with me regularly to talk about the young adult novels she was reading in Spanish at home. I had also read the same novels so we were able to discuss them as fellow readers, sharing our love of books. I found a novel about a political figure in her country who was captured by the Revolutionary Armed Forces of Colombia, *Even Silence Has an End: My Six Years of Captivity in the Colombian Jungle* (Betancourt, 2011). Sara was very excited when I showed her the book in both English and Spanish, stating she wanted me to read it in Spanish, the original language in which it was written, and then ask her questions to clarify what I was reading. She enjoyed helping me make meaning from text through her insider cultural and language knowledge. She read parts of the book in English, but was eager to read the Spanish version once I had finished.

Sharing conversations with students about your mutual reading sends them the message not only that reading is important, but that their response as readers is something you value highly. It allows them a space to be open and ask questions they might be intimidated to ask in front of others. Most important, it can further your relationship, allowing you to get to know them more intimately while sharing about yourself as well.

Presentations

Adolescent English learners also need to practice formal language skills in a safe environment when they are ready. Presentations about their reading are one way of giving them this practice. They can present about a book they read independently or a topic they researched, such as a famous person, through reading various sources by themselves.

For 2 weeks, I helped a group of beginning English learners read multiple texts about a famous person of their choice—Muhammad Ali, Celia Cruz, George Washington, Diego Rivera, and Pelé. They read multiple picture books about the individual in addition to informational text on the Internet, looking for particular information on areas such as the person's cultural and linguistic background, family, accomplishments, obstacles, and legacy. Then, they synthesized their research on posters that contained images and text, which they displayed while presenting to the group using structured sentences that assisted in their speech. To take some of the pressure off the presenter, each person listening needed to ask at least one question. Because students were at the beginning stages of second language development, I provided them a frame for asking and responding to questions. The sentence frames for the audience appear in parenthesis:

- Hello. My name is _____ and I chose to research _____.
- (Where is _____ from?) He/she is from_____.
- (Is he/she alive today?) Yes. He/she is still alive and lives in _____. No. He/she died on _____.
- (Why is he/she famous?) _____ is famous because _____.
- (What is the most interesting fact you learned about _____?) The most interesting fact I learned about _____ is that _____.

These sentence frames gave the presenters and audience ways to engage in conversation in a language they were beginning to learn.

Students with more developed oral language skills can read texts with more complexity and present with more complex sentence frames or none at all. To focus on grammar elements with advanced students, you might use these frames:

- I decided to research _____ because _____.
- (What connections can you make from your life to _____?)
  I am similar to _____ because _____. We have both experienced _____.
- (What would you have done differently during your life if you were _____?) If I were _____ I would (wouldn't) have _____.

- (If you could go back in time and give _____ advice, what would you say to him/her?) I would advise him/her to _____ because he/she _____.

Read Around

Another way to engage students in oral language development through the response to text is the read around (Optiz & Rasinki, 1998), which I have used with ELs in the following way. After engaging in a common text (usually a novel) through shared reading, I ask students to choose a passage from one sentence to a paragraph that resonates with them. They might find the passage meaningful because of the emotion it evoked from them, the beautiful descriptive language, or a connection they have to it. For homework, they need to decide on the passage and prepare to read it out loud, practicing their pronunciation, and hopefully gaining confidence reading orally in English. They also need to prepare to explain to the class or small group why they chose that passage—why it resonated with them. In class the next day, we sit in a circle and each student gets to share the passage meaningful to him or her by reading aloud and then explaining the significance of the passage. Beginning students might just read one sentence and use sentence frames I give them to share why they chose it. More advanced students might read an entire paragraph and then talk for up to 2 minutes on why they chose that passage. This can be a very meaningful way to share how a piece of literature has changed you and is a community-building culminating activity when you finish a longer text.

READER RESPONSE THROUGH WRITTEN LANGUAGE

Just as students should have an opportunity to speak in English every day in your class, they also need regular and varied writing opportunities (Graves, 1983). Writing in response to reading is beneficial because students' reading material can serve as mentor texts (Calkins, 1986) that provide exemplars of how to use certain features of language like descriptive words or how to convey emotion through writing (Culham, 2014). For ELs particularly, mentor texts that share everyday stories from students' cultures send the message that their stories are worthy of being in print, inspiring them to write about their own lives and experiences (Newman, 2012; Stewart, 2015)

Writing from mentor texts could constitute more traditional writing, such as Kelly's students' expository essays on the topic of immigration they read about, but it can also be more informal. Our classroom writing in response to our reading should be diverse. Beginning and intermediate ELs, or even long-term ELs who might be very reluctant writers, need more writing opportunities for fluency rather than accuracy (Fu, 2009). That is, they need to write to develop their thoughts, to use the English language, and to develop the discipline to write for extended amounts of time. Many students have to get over the fear of putting something down on paper. This reluctance to write could be because they are fearful of being graded harshly for their spelling or grammar mistakes, or they might get stuck because they cannot think of a certain word in English when they are not encouraged to use their L1. Perhaps they have never written in any language for extended periods of time and need to develop that stamina. Using multiple methods of reader response through writing can provide daily opportunities for writing fluency as well as opportunities to edit one's writing for accuracy.

Journal Writing

Adolescent ELs need to get in the habit of responding regularly to their reading by writing in a journal (Araujo & Wickstrom, in press). I emphasize to students that this is *their* journal to make meaning from text. I will never grade journal writing for spelling, grammar, or word choice because I do not want students to stop taking necessary risks to produce the output for second language acquisition to occur. They need to regularly use the language they are learning and have a safe space to try out their newly acquired vocabulary or sentence structures. I will also never criticize the content of their journal writing—even if they choose to tell me that they severely dislike the book we read in class. I often tell students to write in any language that they choose and highly encourage them to write in their language at certain times if that will enable them to fully express themselves. However, sometimes I tell them I want them to try to use as much English as they can. If they cannot think of a word in English, I want them to keep writing and put what they need to in their language. A beginning EL might use just a few words in English while a more advanced learner may choose to write the entire response in English.

The goals I have for students' journals are multifaceted, which is why I might have different purposes for different writing assignments, including (1) to develop fluency in L2 writing at any stage of development they are in by giving them a space to produce risk-taking output (Ortega, 2009); (2) to provide an equitable way for them to make meaning from text, encouraging them to respond using their full linguistic repertoire (García et al., 2017); and (3) to engage in regular practices of writing (Graves, 1983).

If students are not used to writing daily in their journals, this can be a difficult practice to implement at first. In a summer class I taught, I quickly realized that the students in the class were not accustomed to writing daily in their classes during the school year. I recognized that I needed to provide more structure to get them to write rather than assigning purely open-ended writing. After a short read-aloud or shared reading, I would place a few prompts on the board and ask students to choose one they would like to answer. This helped most students write in English, their L1, or a mixture of the two for about 5 consecutive minutes each day.

However, two boys in particular would write about 10 words in their journals and tell me they were finished. For many days, after they made their announcement, I would look over their writing and begin asking questions to elicit more detail. I said "more detail" so often, they helped me write it on the board in their language, Burmese, to remind them that they always had more to write, especially if they knew they were not being graded for language or grammar. Every student in the class learned that phrase in Burmese, and I can still remember it exactly from saying it so often and even having it said to me when I needed to explain something better. Eventually, the boys became adept at providing that detail and extending their writing during our regular journal writing. For them, journal writing was like a daily exercise to build stamina as a writer.

Daily journal writing in response to reading is crucial in providing students with a safe space where fluency is the goal and they can explore their thoughts without worrying about accuracy. While engaging in shared reading, I often pause and ask the students to respond in their journals, sometimes giving more structure, such as by asking, "When have you experienced a difficult time in your life such as the character in the book?" Figure 4.1 shows an example of how one student responded to the short story *The Green Armchair* (Ho, 2004) and used this as a space to connect to her reading. She later shared this response orally with the class, creating the atmosphere for other students to share similar connections about speaking English being a difficult obstacle in their lives.

Edmodo or Online Book Discussions

Regular reader response can also occur through collaborative online forums such as Edmodo, which is designed for use in the classroom setting. Dwyer and Larson (2013) illustrate how an online message board can be used to engage adolescents in different countries through a global literature circle where they respond to reading a common text. Online writing offers additional benefits for students learning English, as studies show they use technology to explore and practice their L2 writing (Stewart, 2013; Yi, 2007,

**Figure 4.1. Student Journal Writing in Response *The Green Armchair*
(Ho, 2004)**

Most Hard Time

Hard time I have was Englis because it is hard to read. Some time they have s or not s. It make me so confused. Also they have nan [noun] or verb thing like that. I don't what to do with them. The English have so much rule to speak. They are driving me crazy. I really wanna speak as an American Accent. But it hard to accomplish.

2010). In responding while using a computer, tablet, or cellphone, students can take advantage of the autocorrect features in order to receive immediate feedback on spelling and even some grammatical elements. Online writing also lends itself to conversations between students or student and teacher, much like an interactive writing journal. Because more and more students are online through their cellphones or tablets on a regular basis, online book discussions are ways to continue the conversation beyond the classroom. One student and I had an online conversation about her response to the novel *Wait for Me* (Na, 2006) as she asked for clarification one evening when reading a complicated section in her second language. She wrote: "i hate mina mom cause she is so mena [mean] and she did not like the mexican boy and it ffel me so sad and the korea boy love mina but she did not love her rite [right?]."[3] On my phone that evening, I was able to respond that she had the correct understanding of the story so far and there was a lot of drama in this book.

Although this particular student was obviously not very concerned about writing without errors, I choose not to grade online discussions because I want the goal to be fluency over accuracy. Yet, because this writing is usually shared with others, competent communication is a key element, which means that even though students might not be graded for spelling or grammar, they need to ensure that their writing communicates their desired meaning to the reader. Additionally, as teachers respond to students' reader responses online outside of school, relationships will be strengthened, deepening the community created in R.E.A.L. instruction. Teachers' regular responses also model ways to connect to literature and encourage students to continue their reading outside of school.

Graphic Organizers

Graphic organizers can help ELs make sense of their reading and are useful for comparing and contrasting books, understanding the plot of a story, taking notes while reading informational text, analyzing themes, and examining

---

3. All student writing appears as it was written except where a pseudonym is needed.

the characters (Honigsfeld & Dove, 2013). They provide structure, which is essential for facilitating second language acquisition (Gibbons, 2009); for example, the shape of the outline as well as the formation of the organizer can be used as clues to help students comprehend connections—cause might be a square and effect a circle with arrows that denote which one comes first. Students will revert back to their tables, charts, or thinking maps of important information to help them understand important elements of their reading, further supporting comprehensible input as they progress through the text or prepare to complete an activity about their reading.

Graphic organizers also provide differentiation that supports classrooms with ELs of varying English language levels. I often modify graphic organizers in classes, asking more advanced students to provide more detail. For instance, I might give a very new student a character analysis graphic organizer with only four shapes to fill in, which might require a lot of time if the student needs to locate those descriptive words in English. However, in reading the same text, I might give students with more English development a more detailed graphic organizer that provides many shapes, indicating more information they will need to glean from the text about the character's physical appearance, emotions, desires, and actions. The simpler structure can allow a beginning student to respond with only a few words, while more advanced students can respond with longer ideas and more specific details. In large mixed-level classes, teachers can use the graphic organizer as the end product for beginning students and a springboard to a larger product, such as an essay for more advanced students.

Edited and Published Pieces

Publishing a piece of writing gives the activity more meaning because students have an actual audience to write for rather than just the teacher (Cloud et al., 2010). Publishing student writing does not actually mean you need to find a publishing company; it can be something the teacher does with her students. Marie asked her students to submit their poetry for a class book she printed for each student that contained what students believed to be their best work. Other teachers have their students publish writing online on websites that regularly share student writing. Susan even published her newest student, José's, short essay of his adventure, coming from Venezuela to the United States (see Figure 4.2) by displaying it in the school hallway on a poster he made about his country. He knew that his audience was other students and teachers in the school who would walk by and see his work.

Edited or published writing can be a culminating project that results from students' previous informal writing. For example, I often have students select one of their reader response entries in their journals that they want to further develop. They choose what is important to them that they want to share with others through writing. Then, I will provide an appropriate graphic organizer to help them further develop this idea.

Figure 4.2. Beginning Student's First Published Writing in His New School

My Adventure

I am from Venezuela. I came here by plane, because my country is not good standing but I came for a better education and better life. In Venezuela there is no food, nothing is easy to get. Government is bad, I hate the government from Venezuela. I went to the airport in my father's truck, listening to music. I was going to leave my family.

Once students have planned their poem or essay on their graphic organizers, they begin by writing a rough draft where they will pay more attention to accuracy—correct spelling, word choice, and grammar. I might guide them to focus on a special area such as subject/verb agreement through a mini-lesson on that topic. Through a writer's workshop (Calkins, 1986), students will meet with me or with other students in the class to decide which revisions need to be made to their rough drafts over the course of a few days. I usually meet with students individually or in small groups multiple times to help them with specific elements of their writing. At the end, we read the writing for final editing, looking for any errors or something that needs to be changed. The final copy is then saved for an anthology of classroom writing or published immediately through an online source. Because students know that their writing will be shared with others, they take special ownership of it.

While I was helping Aye Cho Htay with her migration essay in response to reading books about the refugee experience, I realized how important this essay was to her because she was going to share it with others—specifically, other teachers who did not know her story. This essay explained how she fled her country to go to a refugee camp in Thailand and then, after many years, finally resettled in the United States. In the essay, she explains all the negative things that kept happening to her family. I encouraged her to change her title, "My Journey of Hope and Peace," to more closely match the content from my perspective. However, she was very passionate about her title and explained to me that she viewed all the negative instances as a journey of hope and peace because of her faith. As a writer, she had a message she wanted to send the reader and she was intent on conveying that message. (See Figure 4.3 for an excerpt from Aye Cho Htay's essay.)

The publishing process, sharing her migration story from her perspective with teachers and fellow students, gave her more stake in the writing. She knew we would be reading her personal narrative, including the title, and thus, she was likely more adamant to communicate her message, even though I mistakenly suggested that she change the title and send a different message to the reader. I think that if this narrative writing had been a regular assignment where only I read it and returned it to her with a grade, she would have easily gone along with my suggestions.

Figure 4.3. Excerpt of Student Essay Published in Anthology in Response to Reading on Immigration

My Journey of Hope and Peace

I remember one time when I was in Burma in the evening when we started to eat and put the rice on our plates, we heard the gun shots. Then, we didn't eat anymore. We ran away because the Burmese and Karen soldiers were fighting near my village. All the people in my village were scared and they could not sleep that night. The next morning, I heard that a lot of Karen soldiers had died so we didn't live there anymore. We sold all of our land so we could get money. We went to Thailand in a boat. The people who came after us told us that nobody was living in our village. The village looked like a forest.

Then we had very hard times. When we were new in Thailand we stayed in my grandfather's home for a few days. The people from the UN told us to go to the refugee camp office. They asked us about what happened in Burma and then they took a UN picture of us. Then, we lived in the refugee camp in Thailand for four years. The people who worked at the UN came and asked about my granddad because he had lived in Thailand for a long time. He came before we came. Then the UN asked why he didn't go to America. We told them it was because he lived with his niece. My granddad also could not talk because he was born deaf and mute. He always wanted to live with us. Whenever he had the opportunity to come to America, he wanted to wait on us. Then the people from the UN understood. My granddad wanted his niece, my mom, to go to America with him. The truth is, we wouldn't have come to the U.S.A., if it weren't for my granddad.

We waited in Thailand for two years, and then we came to America. When we left the refugee camp, we stayed in Masaw, Thailand for one week. I felt so sad because my mom got an eye infection and my sister was also pregnant. If women are very pregnant or if you are sick, they do not let you come to the U.S.A. They send you back to the refugee camp. I thought I would have to go back to the camp. That night before we went to sleep, we prayed to God that we could come to America. On the last day they said we could go to America. In the morning we went to the airport and we went to America.

When we got to America, it was so different for me and I was so sad. At night I couldn't sleep because it was daytime in Asia.

Like Aye Cho Htay, ELs often have much they want to share with others about themselves, their identities, or their opinions, and we need them to correct our faulty assumptions or lack of understanding, as illustrated through my experience with her. Writing for an authentic audience is an effective way of helping students take ownership of their learning and see the relevance in the assignment. As students genuinely want to engage in the writing process—planning, drafting, revising, editing, and publishing—in response to and as mentored by their reading, they will develop literacy skills as well as further their second language acquisition.

READER RESPONSE THROUGH OTHER CREATIVE METHODS

Responding through the arts is particularly useful for ELs to respond to literature in a way that furthers their second language acquisition and biliteracy development and provides them more equity to express their ideas (Chappel & Faltis, 2013). Often, ELs will feel frustration in classes that require English language proficiency in order to be successful. Using the arts gives them access to a way to express their learning that is not embedded in any specific language, such as English. This creative outlet can provide students with a chance to tap into their full understanding and higher-order thinking capacity to more completely demonstrate their learning, unlimited by their emergent English skills.

Visual Art

In order for students to respond to a text using a form of visual art, they need to comprehend the text deeply, which will develop their overall literacy skills and second language abilities if they are reading in English. Once they have created their response product, they will need to use their oral language or writing skills to explain how their piece of art connects to the text.

For example, in one class I taught during the summer, I had no computers or art supplies available from the school. I had to be resourceful, so I brought poster board, used magazines, and colored paper from my house and borrowed my own children's markers, glue, and scissors. In essence, I had nothing fancy—all items that could be purchased very inexpensively at a grocery store. This small and unimpressive supply of art utensils was expertly used by students to respond to literature. In response to reading various books about the refugee experience, a student named Than drew a scene from his own journey of migration. Without any prompting from me, he took one green sheet of computer paper and created a scene of his family hiding in the woods as they crossed through Thailand as undocumented migrants to get to the refugee camp in Malaysia. Figure 4.4 demonstrates how he drew his family in pencil and did not color them in like the other parts of the scene to illustrate that they were trying to be invisible during this time in his life as they hid from the Thai police. He developed his literacy skills through this project by reading about other refugee youth and then explaining his drawing to me and others while stating the connections he had to particular texts we read. At the end of this unit, Than had used English, Burmese, and Chin to discuss his artwork and literary connections.

Figure 4.4. Student Drawing in Response to Reading About Immigration

The student drew the scenery with vibrantly colored markers, yet the people are sketched in pencil, illustrating that they wanted to be hidden from the Thai police.

Comics

Asking students to respond to class reading by creating comics taps into students' artistic abilities to convey meaning with purposeful yet limited text. Comics require fewer words than books to convey a narrative, allowing ELs to think deeply about grammar and word choice for their captions. Teachers can provide a language focus for the assignment—for example, using descriptive language to build vocabulary or focus on grammar such as irregular past tense verbs (*went, left, came, hid, rode*). In addition to honing language skills when creating comics, students can also can use skills that are not language embedded to creatively use drawing or graphic art to convey meaning. I encourage teachers to use many graphic novels as mentor texts to discuss how the visuals support the language. Show students the entire book or single pages from the graphic novel *El Deafo* (Bell & Lasky, 2014), which expertly uses imagery and shapes to inform the reader what the main character (who is deaf) understands as opposed to what someone has said out loud.

Students can illustrate scenes from their own lives that relate to their reading, or they can portray events from the literature they are reading to further understand the plot. The comic creator at www.readwritethink.org

provides a structured graphic organizer to help students effectively plan each scene. Two students used this graphic organizer before creating their graphic representations of their migration experience in response to their reading. (See Figure 4.5 to see the differing products from using the comic creator.) This activity fostered reading skills as students read about others' migration experiences and used critical thinking skills in planning each visual and line of text. Finally, they developed their writing skills by working with me to edit each sentence to accompany the visuals.

Theater

In Marie's class, intermediate ELs responded to the book *Novio Boy* (Soto, 2006), which is a lighthearted play about the sometimes awkward and funny moments in teenage romance. The play is written in English, but because the characters are mainly bilingual, there are many phrases in Spanish as well. The students responded to this work by writing a script that extends the story, staying true to the characters' personalities and important events in the book. The students worked together in small groups to create and perform their scenes. One group of students creatively used dialogue in the same way that the original book did—mixing English and Spanish. They noticed how, in the book, not all the Spanish was proper, so they inventively wrote a line in the script with a word in Spanish that does not actually exist in an official Spanish dictionary, but reflects how some Spanish speakers use language, particularly in the United States. In place of the official term for "driver's test," *examen de manejo*, they used the term *examen de manejación*, expertly using critical-thinking skills to extend the story. The difference between the two phrases is what some Spanish speakers, such as the students in this group from Colombia, Mexico, and Puerto Rico, might consider "correct Spanish" as opposed to what these students had heard American-born Spanish speakers use for the same concept—driver's test. Another group began their scene 10 years later, demonstrating much creativity and critical thinking in using textual evidence to consider what each character would be doing a decade after the text ended. The literacy skills that each group used in this response activity entailed writing their scripts using a specific genre, the play, and then reading and performing them after much practice with pronunciation, fluency, pauses, and voice inflections in their groups. They also had to revert back to the original work, which they had read as a class, to stay true to the characters the author had created.

EVALUATING STUDENTS' RESPONSES

Responding in community to meaningful works will be demanding, but it should be what reveals humanity (Christensen, 2009), drawing a class together through the shared human experience. Because of this great potential of responding within a community, you need to ensure that you are not

Figure 4.5. Students' Illustrated Migration Experience with Different Artistic Visuals and Text

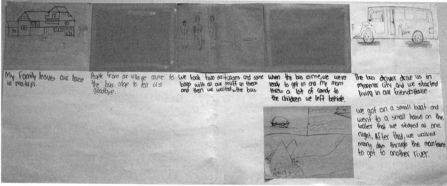

lessening students' reading and responding by "over-grading." For example, I have seen students only read in order to complete the written response activity they need for a grade. They read for the necessary information and then stop, rarely finishing a book or engaging deeply with the content. If receiving a grade is the goal of reader response products, much can be lost, such as comprehension, a deep understanding of the text, and meaningful connections.

However, most classrooms require grades, which are usually assigned by evaluating the products that students create. Therefore, final products such as essays or presentations might have a rubric used for grading them, but daily journal writing should be celebrated as an expression of learning rather than a formal assessment. Reading students' written responses can be an excellent way to informally assess their engagement with their reading—is it intellectually rigorous or is it only at the surface level? Teachers can also informally assess students through other daily reader response activities, such as talking with partners, group discussion, or making graphic organizers. Most important, be vigilant that grading does not extinguish your students' reading and responding to texts in meaningful ways. This is a crucial area where you will need to remember your simple rules and take adaptive action when needed to change common patterns of students completing work just to get grades. Consider award-winning high school ELA teacher Linda Christensen's (2009) grading policy, which includes several criteria, such as students' completion of homework, classwork, and participation in class. What it does not include are grades in the traditional sense. She explains: "I discovered early on that if I wanted to produce writers I needed to let go of grades" (p. 272). She expertly and explicitly teaches how to write in different genres, gives mini-lessons, holds conferences with students, and helps them make revisions. She gives students points for their drafts and revisions, but there is never a final grade on an individual piece of writing because she does not want the students to ever think it is finished; in doing so, she models the idea that writing is a process. Her students will complete many drafts of a writing assignment because they care about the content.

If that is too big of a jump to make, consider using Kelly Gallagher's (2009) short responses that call for deep thinking about a text in order to hold students responsible for their reading. Continually search for ideas of ways to hold students accountable and complete your responsibilities for giving them a grade if required while not killing their reading or willingness to respond.

ACTION TIME

- Think about your classroom discussions. Does everyone have the opportunity to participate? Try partner conversations with the Numbered Heads Together strategy available at this site: https://www.teachervision.com/group-work/numbered-heads-together-cooperative-learning-strategy

- Schedule individual meetings with students to talk about what you are both reading in and out of the class.

- Visit www.readwritethink.org to search for graphic organizers you can use to help students respond to literature.

- Set up an Edmodo account (at www.edmodo.com) to engage your students in book discussions online.

- Read the following books for more ideas of how you can incorporate the arts into your ESL or ELA curriculum.

  ✓ Landay, E., Wootton, K., & Heath, S. B. (2012). *A reason to read: Linking literacy and the arts.* Cambridge, MA: Harvard Education Press.

  ✓ Chappell, S. V., & Faltis, C. (2013). *The arts and emergent bilingual youth: Building culturally responsive, critical and creative education in school and community contexts.* New York, NY: Routledge.

CHAPTER 5

Connect to Students' Cultures and Lived Experiences

Susan is a high school teacher who has taught English language arts for many years, but she is new to teaching English learners and open to learning new ideas to help them develop their second language literacy. I get to work with her high school ESL class, which has students at many different English language levels and from various countries. Two of these students are Esnad, a Palestinian from Jordan, and Koen, who is from Laos and prefers to be called "Big Papi." Neither student knows very much about the other's culture, and Susan doesn't know very much about these students' countries or cultures either—at least, not yet. In order to learn about her students, she locates literature that represents each student's culture or country and uses these books for whole-class and individual reading during a 4-week unit, Where I'm From and Who I Am. Using many forms of literacy (writing, speaking, and representing), students share selected elements about their countries and cultural backgrounds through essays, artwork, and poetry. Esnad and Koen write bilingual poetry in English and their home languages (Arabic and Lao) that describes the landscape of their countries as well as its food, sounds, and people. They make artistic collages that display their countries' flags and other elements that remind them of home, including written narratives that share information about their religion and traditions. Through connecting literacy to her students' cultural heritages, Susan learns a great deal about her students, providing them with an authentic reason to share about themselves through art, writing, and speaking.

Literacy is how we learn about others and share our lives. We privilege students' knowledge when it becomes essential to our classroom curriculum, acknowledging that each student possesses unique, culturally embedded knowledge that we might not possess ourselves. Using this knowledge as a foundation and source of academic learning can lead to greater literacy gains, particularly in the L2 (González et al., 2005). This is a great strength to the ELA or ESL classroom. As teachers become learners of students' lives, the need for authentic uses of literacy arises. Students will be more motivated to write and speak when they know that you and the other learners in the classroom want to know about their area of expertise—their culture.

A HOLISTIC VIEW OF CULTURE

But what is one's culture? Because this is an abstract concept, we are apt to focus on the more visible and tangible parts of culture that are often referred to as surface culture. Using Hall's (1976) analogy of the iceberg, the surface features of culture are only a small part of what is really there. The superficial elements of culture are important to note, but they cannot be confused with the deeper elements. These features are sometimes referred to "the Fs" in the study of multicultural education: food, famous people, festivals, flags, folklore, and fashion. Many researchers call upon educators to move beyond these surface features (Bennett, 2015; Nieto & Bode, 2012), which can lead to overgeneralizations, false assumptions, and even negative stereotypes.

Nieto and Bode (2012) explain that a more holistic definition of culture gives educators a more effective way to view their students:

> Culture consists of the values, traditions, worldview, and social and political relations created, shared, and transformed by a group of people bound together by a common history, geographic location, language, social class, religion, or other shared identity. (p. 158)

Below the iceberg is where most of one's cultural identity will reside. This includes one's attitude, worldview, communication style, values, moral code, beliefs on age or gender roles, preference regarding physical space, and family relationships. Certainly, cultural identity is complex, and adolescent English learners might feel they are members of more than one cultural group based on their home country, primary language, new country, age, or another affinity group, such as fans of manga or soccer. Teachers can use this complex notion of culture to allow students to use various forms of literacy to investigate, contemplate, and share their own culture. Although "the Fs," surface culture, can be included in cultural explorations, elements of deeper culture should also be considered. Bennett (2015) asks educators to consider these questions when thinking about deep culture:

- What is your view of time? Is it fixed or loose? If an event is scheduled to begin at 5:00, what time do you arrive?
- How do you deliver verbal messages? Do you use direct speech that gets to the point, or do you extend your speech with extra language?
- What are the social roles to which you adhere? Consider gender, familial, and age distinctions.
- How do you greet someone? How much space do you prefer between you and a stranger? Is that the same with friends or family members? Does this differ by someone's gender or age?
- With adolescents, it is especially important to consider what constitutes adulthood in a particular culture. How are young people expected to act toward people in authority and to one another? What

are dating and marriage norms in particular cultures? When is one considered an adult? What does adulthood entail?

These are just some of the many questions to consider as we implement R.E.A.L. instruction in our classrooms. As you begin this ongoing conversation with students, more elements of their cultural heritage will emerge, providing fertile soil for literacy development.

With a holistic understanding of culture, we can better understand why Angela Valenzuela (1999) writes about the need for a culture-affirming curriculum. Our students need to know that we acknowledge them as cultural beings and we value their uniqueness. But what does that look like? How can we affirm students' cultures within our classrooms? Richard Ruiz (1997) explains that the curriculum should not just include students' culture, but that students' culture should be the curriculum. This is especially true for English learners in their reading because the more connections a reader can make to the text, the greater the literacy gains that will be possible, especially in the L2 (Ebe, 2012). This also communicates to students that they matter and have something to offer the classroom (Newman, 2012). The teacher and other students will not possess the same cultural knowledge; consequently, each student's unique contributions are important. The Action Time section at the end of this chapter includes activities you can do with your students to begin learning *from* them about their cultures and lives.

READING AND RESPONDING WITH CULTURAL INSIDERS

There are many facets and nuances to culture, and it might be overwhelming to think of all of them at one time. Countries can be a good place to start because students will often possess much knowledge about their country or their parents' country that others do not possess, creating an authentic reason for them to use their emerging English skills to share with the teacher and others. In order to reap the benefits of reading and responding to texts with students who have insider knowledge, you must first have literature and other texts about every country, culture, and **people group** represented in the class (plus others) that are accessible for all ELs' English levels, yet still appropriate for older learners. That is why, when I first begin to work with a new group of ELs, I make sure I have literature that represents each student. The box (Websites for Information on Specific Regions) on the following page illustrates websites I use to help me locate books and other supporting materials on specific regions. These sites help me identify poetry, short stories, picture books, and novels that I can use in the classroom through various reading methods (read-aloud, shared, guided, close, or independent reading). Some books and online materials serve as resources for students to conduct research. Even information they already know about their country is beneficial when they see it presented in English, and there is always more history they can learn. I have

---

WEBSITES FOR INFORMATION ON SPECIFIC REGIONS

- wowlit.org – Search for literature within a specific region or country. In the search box, you can type the country name.
- Eastwestdiscoverypress.com – This publisher has children's and adolescent books in more than 50 languages. The site can assist you in locating literature about specific countries or regions in various languages.
- kids.nationalgeographic.com/world – On this site, students can use the interactive map to explore various countries. Many different countries and regions will appear for multimodal information about that location.
- http://rebeccahinsonpublishing.com/books.html – These books take a deep look at history through art from different cultures, countries, and regions, and are published in many different languages.

---

also used books with adolescent ELs from the series listed in Table 5.1 that includes visually rich texts about specific countries, regions, or people groups. The box (Additional Books about Specific Countries or Regions) after Table 5.1 provides individual book titles about specific countries that portray positive aspects as well as controversial issues. Sometimes I'll use one of these books as a read-aloud and ask the student with the insider knowledge beforehand if he or she would be willing to share about parts of the book we might not understand as well as the student does. I also provide some of these books for independent reading, and students regularly gravitate toward books about their own countries and then toward those about the countries of their friends in the class.

Remembering "Home" Through Books

The place we grew up that sets the background for our childhood memories is often what we refer to as "home." Newcomer adolescents have received most of their education and socialization in another country, and even ELs who have lived in the United States for many years might maintain connections to their country of birth or their parents' country through technology, news, family, and even visits. Campano & Ghiso (2011) state we should view these students as cosmopolitan intellectuals because of the factual and experiential knowledge they have regarding a place about which the teacher and other members of the class might know very little.

I was meeting with Nathan regularly to discuss his reading, and one day, I brought him a new book I had just received. He immediately said, "This is my country! This is my country, Miss!" when he realized that the graphic

Table 5.1. Book Series About Specific Countries

Series Title	Publisher	Special Features	Countries, Regions, or Cities in Series
Country Explorers	Lerner	Real photographs with easy-to-read factual information; accessible to beginning ELs	Chile, China, Costa Rica, Cuba, Germany, Ghana, Guatemala, Iceland, Indonesia, Iran, Ireland, Italy, Jamaica, Madagascar, New Zealand, Norway, Pakistan, Philippines, Poland, Puerto Rico, Russia, Saudi Arabia, South Korea, Tanzania, Turkey, United Kingdom
I See the Sun	Satya House Publications	Artistic illustrations made from collages of photographs, paper cutouts, and drawings; bilingual in English and the most common language of the country featured	Myanmar, Mexico, Russia, Afghanistan, China, Nepal
Global Hotspots	Marshall Cavendish Children's Books	Historical and modern information for older readers that covers complex situations in these countries	Burma (Myanmar), Colombia, Cuba, Iraq, Iran, Israel and Palestine, North Korea, Tibet, the Indian Subcontinent, Sudan, Zimbabwe
ThingsAsian Kids	ThingsAsian Press	Bilingual in English and the primary language of the region; rich illustrations by artists who are from or reside in that country	Myanmar, Indonesia, Bangkok, Mongolia, Hanoi, Hong Kong, Tokyo

---

ADDITIONAL BOOKS ABOUT SPECIFIC COUNTRIES OR REGIONS

Wells, R., & Yoshi. (1992). *A to Zen: A book of Japanese culture.* New York, NY: Simon & Schuster. Opening right to left, like a book in Japanese, each letter represents a term to describe Japanese culture. The word is also written in Japanese, accompanied by a paragraph of text and illustration.

Feelings, M. L., & Feelings, T. (1974). *Jambo means hello: Swahili alphabet book.* New York, NY: Dial Press. Each page could stand alone in this picture book that provides a Swahili word and cultural explanation for each letter of the alphabet. There are people who speak Swahili from the following countries: Kenya, Tanzania, Zanzibar, Uganda, Democratic Republic of Congo, Zambia, Mozambique, Malawi, Rwanda, Burundi, Somalia, and the Comoro Islands.

Rubin, S. G. (2013). *Diego Rivera: An artist for the people.* New York, NY: Abrams Books for Young Readers. Tonatiuh, D., & Rivera, D. (2011). *Diego Rivera: His world and ours.* New York, NY: Abrams Books for Young Readers. Winter, J., & Juan, A. (2002). *Frida.* New York, NY: Arthur A. Levine. These three books explore Mexican history through famous artists. The first book contains Rivera's artwork while sharing his life and important elements of Mexico's culture and history. The second book explains the political and cultural importance of Rivera's murals. Students can also study Mexican history through reading limited text accompanied by vibrant illustrations in the third book about Frida Kahlo.

Miller, R. J. (2013). *A humble village.* Lexington, KY: Robin Joyce Miller. The book contains very limited text perfect for beginning ELs and rich illustrations about a Ugandan village.

Rodger, E. (2017). *Leaving my homeland: A refugee's journey from the Democratic Republic of the Congo.* Ontario, Canada: Crabtree Publishing Company. Pictures, charts, maps, and graphs along with one child's personal story make this a compelling book for ELs of many language levels. I wish I would have had this book when working with Camille mentioned in Chapter 1.

Venkatraman, P. (2014). *A time to dance.* New York, NY: Speak. This is a story told in verse about a dancer trained in the traditional Indian *Bharatanatyam.* The book is filled with many elements of the rich and varied cultures of India.

---

novel I gave him, *Child Soldier: When Boys and Girls Are Used in War* (Chikwanine & Humphreys, 2015), was about what occurred in his country, the Democratic Republic of the Congo. He found the map in the book and spent many minutes explaining to me the places where he and his family had lived and where his great grandparents were from. Through this explanation about his country, I learned how his father and uncle had been persecuted because of their Rwandan descent, causing them to flee for their lives and seek refugee status. This led Nathan to explain how his last name, which denoted his Rwandan roots, caused his mother to fear for his life when he was younger and how he eventually came to join his father in the United States. What began as an explanation of events in his country led to a detailed history of his family that told me a lot about this young man.

Camille was also born in the DRC and, although she had lived in many different countries in Africa, she proudly told me that the DRC was *her* country. After I included a text called *The Democratic Republic of the Congo in Pictures* (DiPiazza, 2008) in our classroom library, she took the book home every day for a month, always bringing it back to class and often choosing to read it during independent reading time. I found out later that she had been copying every word from the book at home in her writing journal, illustrating her emotional connection to her country. Although she rarely spoke in class, she began to use the pictures in the book to tell me different things about her country, and later on, her life. When I told her she could keep the book, she beamed.

Unfortunately, Camille and Nathan were not in the same school and did not get to share insider information with each other about the texts they read about their countries. However, when you do have the opportunity to teach students from the same country or even region, letting them work collaboratively to teach you about their country and explain the differences in the regions can be an excellent activity to develop their L2 literacy skills. For example, in a summer literacy institute I taught a group of multileveled Burmese students. I knew very little about their country and customs, and particularly, the uniqueness of their people groups within the same country. They worked cooperatively to teach me about their country, speaking in English to communicate with me, in Burmese to communicate with one another, and even in the regional languages of Karen and Chin to speak within small groups or partners. We read *I See the Sun in Myanmar (Burma)* (King, 2014) and *M Is for Myanmar* (Rush, 2011) together through read-alouds, and some students also chose to read these books again individually to develop ideas on specific cultural elements that they wanted to share more about through essays, poetry, presentations, art, or informal conversation. Then, because I did not have books on their specific people groups (Zo, Tedim, Chin, and Karen), they searched the Internet for online texts and visuals to explain their specific uniqueness.

Through their sharing, I learned that some of these students preferred not to identify as Burmese, but rather by the name of their specific people group. Student Mya Day wanted to write her final essay from the summer institute about a leader of her people group because the day the Karen people celebrate him fell on a school day and she wanted to celebrate with us. She researched the information online and determined the English words to use to teach the class about this special day for the Karen people. She then contributed an essay about her people group's hero, Saw Ba Oo Gyi, to our class anthology and explained to the entire class, even the other Burmese students who were not in her people group, why August 12 is a special day for the Karen people.

Mya Day taught me it is important that we do not make large assumptions about students based on the country they or their parents are from. Sometimes their identity and loyalty will be more tied to a people group than to a common nationality. Encouraging students who are from particular people groups to share that with you and the class affirms their culture in a way they will not be accustomed to in the United States, because we usually equate national origin with culture. Acknowledging that students' culture is more complex than just their nationality will show them that you want to learn about them as they share with you.

Presenting About a Country

Giving a formal presentation in a middle or high school classroom can be difficult—especially in your second language. After working with one group of newcomer high school students who were very timid to speak in English, I wanted to create a safe space for them to begin to use oral English. I began a month-long activity to guide them in making a presentation about their own country. First, we read books about various countries together through shared reading; I read aloud and the students followed along by sharing a copy between two people. Together, we created a simple graphic organizer for each country by writing the country's name in the center of the paper and drawing four quadrants around it. We determined what to label each quadrant based on what information we were learning about the country, such as language, cultural traditions, geography, animals, climate, and so on. After repeating this reading and responding activity a few times to create familiarity with the recurring vocabulary, I provided students with literature about their own countries and asked them to make their own graphic organizer with the information they wanted to share. When the students finished the graphic organizer, I gave them sentence frames to scaffold them in telling the others in the group certain facts about their country. I also provided the group with sentence frames to help them ask questions, requiring each student to ask at least one question of the presenter, which got everyone involved in structured oral language practice. Below are some examples of those sentence frames:

For the Presenter:

- I am from _____.
- In my country, most people speak _____.
- A common food is _____.
- Some of the animals that inhabit my country are _____.

For the Audience:

- What animals are in your country?
- What is your favorite food from your country?
- What is an important holiday in your country?
- How do you celebrate this special holiday?
- What colors are on the flag?

This is an activity to scaffold beginners' emergent oral language use or to help those students who are progressing well in reading, writing, and listening but are still reluctant to speak. As students develop more language skills, they can use their graphic organizer research to create posters or digital presentations so they can present for a larger group in a more formal setting. If they engage in filling out their graphic organizer, making a poster, and a digital presentation, they will have many opportunities to develop their vocabulary using writing, art, and technology, each time growing more comfortable speaking in English and using more vocabulary and grammatical structures.

Sharing and Learning About One's Heritage

Certainly, not all ELs are from other countries, yet they will probably have at least one parent from another country and will be aware of cultural elements within that country, making them cultural insiders. In Susan's class, Ben, although he was born in the United States, used his writing and art to teach us about his parents' country, Puerto Rico, during Susan's Where I'm From and Who I Am unit. He also became our cultural insider as the class read about people of Puerto Rican heritage, such as Supreme Court Justice Sonia Sotomayor, in the books *Sonia Sotomayor: A Judge Grows in the Bronx* (Winter, Rodriguez, & Palacios, 2009) and *Sonia Sotomayor: Supreme Court Justice* (Bernier-Grand & Gonzalez, 2010). When we came to words in the text in Spanish that none of the other Spanish speakers from Mexico or South America understood, such as *mofongo*, Ben proudly described the typical Puerto Rican dish, how it was made, and traditional times to eat it. He brought in memories from his family life as he spoke to the class in English about cultural norms and celebrations. He was the class's cultural insider while reading this literature, enthusiastically stopping me at certain places in the reading so he could share something to help us further comprehend the texts, demonstrating his pride in his cultural heritage.

Other ELs might want to investigate their cultural roots to understand their parents and grandparents better and to build cross-generational connections. Campano (2007) writes about how his urban 5th-graders from many different linguistic, cultural, and ethnic backgrounds engaged in authentic literacy activities through researching and sharing their own families' stories. Students interviewed their older family members to learn more about their countries of origin and migration stories. They engaged in intergenerational storytelling, using all of their languages, and shared those stories with the learning community. They also wrote narratives to remember their family history, entailing their families' story of survival and migration, and they used the arts through the pictures and drama they employed to tell their stories. The students' cultures essentially became the literacy curriculum in this multiethnic and multilinguistic classroom, illustrating the many literacy learning possibilities through enacting a similar project.

This is relevant because, often at the secondary level, we struggle to encourage family engagement or parent involvement with our teaching, especially for immigrant parents (Turney & Kao, 2009). However, parents and adult family members can play a crucial role in students' education regardless of whether they speak English or not. Using family members' histories and knowledge will be beneficial for both native- and foreign-born ELs and provide an avenue to involve parents in their child's education. Learning about one's cultural heritage in order to share it with the class through speaking, writing, and the arts is an authentic way to promote English development, but students also hone their L1 abilities as they interview family members.

Poetry as Mentor Texts

More advanced English learners can use poetry as mentor texts to write about their culture as they practice figurative language, alliteration, or new vocabulary. Acrostic poems help students think deeply about word choice, particularly descriptive words. I have read *Many Luscious Lollipops* (Heller, 1992) to get students to develop a list of adjectives they can use to describe different people or places they are familiar with in order to develop their vocabulary. Students can use *African Acrostics: A Word in Edgeways* (Harley & Noyes, 2009) as a mentor text that will provide examples of how they might write their own acrostic poems by using their name, people group, country, language, or hobbies. This is a great activity to help students be purposeful in their use of adjectives to describe what they know, and it can be modified easily for difficulty level. Figure 5.1 displays a student's biographical acrostic poem about his people group, the Chin people of Myanmar.

Some anthologies of poetry can be used as mentor texts to illustrate how to express emotion through words. Some poems put into words students' feelings about their bilingualism and biculturalism, such as *Cool Salsa: Bilingual Poems on Growing up Hispanic in the United States* (Carlson, 2013). Other poems might tie into elements of students' cultures, including popular culture or youth culture from the book *Poetry Speaks Who I Am: Poems of Discovery,*

Figure 5.1. Student's Biographical Acrostic Poem

Culture of the people in western Myanmar

Has 65 different groups of people

Includes Matupi, Zo, Turg, Teddim, Falam, and Mizo

New Year's is always celebrated by the lunar calendar

Inspiration, and Independence and Everything Else (Paschen & Raccah, 2010). This collection of poems provides examples of poetry from various cultures and experiences to help students use poetry to express who they are.

If students are reluctant to write poetry or do not know where to start, you might use George Ella Lyon's (1999) "Where I'm From" poem to provide scaffolding for students to write about their own cultural heritage. If you use this activity when you begin to get to know your students, it can provide great information to use in your curriculum—like an overview of an individual student's cultural heritage. (See Figure 5.2 for an example of a student's "Where I'm From" poem.) It can provide ideas on what to explore in the future while also preventing the teacher from perpetuating untrue stereotypes or assumptions of students. For example, after Khin wrote his "Where I'm From" poem, I knew that his family was devoutly Christian, which was beneficial when I later read the class a picture book that portrayed people from his country as Buddhists. I was able to say before I read the book that I knew not all of the information represented him and I asked him to show me and the class what was different about his experiences.

To put this into practice, use close reading to analyze Lyon's (1999) "Where I'm From" poem (available at her website, http://www.georgeellalyon.com/where.html). Provide students with sentence frames that can also be found on Lyon's website to write their own poems and make sure you write your own poem as well to share with students. You can publish the final products in a class anthology or create posters with each poem, using art to enhance students' presentation of themselves and their cultural heritage.

Figure 5.2. "Where I'm From" Poem of a Student from Vietnam

I am from the back of the curtain,
From Dad's coffee and Mom's cooking.
I am from the gold fishes in the roof-top aquarium
(Yellow, sparkling, they look like pearls.)
I am from the flowers in different kinds,
whom will just be ephemeral,
wonder if that will be my life.
I'm from the wood and dark brown eyes,
from Ahn and those names that are hard to say.
I'm from everything-is-neat,
and you have to make-it-strict.
From just do it, don't talk back!
I'm from pagoda and from the teaching of Buddha,
like what my mom always said that everything brings karma.
I'm from Nguyễn and Phạm's Branch,
sticky rice and sausage on the top.
From the scratch in my father's back, when he worked so hard
to hold the family not to fall apart
and mom's lullaby was calming us down.
From the calendar that was hanging on the wall,
to the frames on the case.
Time passes like winds blow, people are changing,
but their smiles are still the same.
Growing and faded by time,
hanging on the tree,
a leaf knew its destiny . . .
but not to be wasted away.

PRIVILEGING STUDENTS' LIVED EXPERIENCES

Lived experiences provide one's firsthand accounts of the world. These are events in which individuals have participated that define how they see the world. Our collective lived experiences—positive, negative, and everything in between—form our personality, opinions, skills, worldview, and ideas. Because my students' lived experiences are uniquely theirs, they will have special connections to texts and knowledge that they can teach me and others.

It is very beneficial to purposefully select reading that privileges students' lived experiences or their Homeplace Position in order for them to have more meaningful interactions with a text (Brooks & Browne, 2012). The beauty of making students' experiences a central part of our reading curriculum is that as we begin to learn more and more about our students, we can be more equipped to select texts that privilege their knowledge. Simply put, a snowball effect can occur—the more we know, the better we get at selecting literacy activities to learn even more from our students.

It's important to position yourself as a learner and listen to the students' responses while reading these texts to learn from them and allow their unique experiences to shine. The following box (Suggested Texts to Possibly Connect to Students' Culturally Embedded Experiences) provides some examples of texts that ELs I worked with connected to through their culturally

SUGGESTED TEXTS TO POSSIBLY CONNECT TO STUDENTS' CULTURALLY EMBEDDED EXPERIENCES

Danticat, E., & Staub, L. (2015). *Mama's nightingale: A story of immigration and separation*. New York, NY: Dial Books for Young Readers. Picture book that illustrates experiences of family separation because of immigration and living with undocumented parents.

Brown, S. (2014). *Caminar*. Somerville, MA: Candlewick Press. Novel in verse that illustrates experiences living in a war zone, facing difficult decisions, and bravery.

De la Cruz, M. (2005). *Fresh off the boat*. New York, NY: HarperCollins. Young adult novel that illustrates the experience of negotiating cultural differences of friends and parents and living as an undocumented immigrant with humor.

Yoon, N. (2016). *The sun is also a star*. New York, NY: Delacorte Press. Young adult novel that explores the experience of dating someone of a different race/culture.

Na, A. (2016). *A step from heaven* (1st Atheneum paperback ed.). New York, NY: Simon & Schuster. Novel written in vignettes about the Korean immigrant experience and parent/child negotiations.

Ada, A. F., & Zubizarreta, G. M. (2011). *Dancing home*. New York, NY: Atheneum Books for Young Readers. Middle grade novel (also available in Spanish) that explores feelings of pride and shame for one's cultural heritage.

McCall, G. G. (2012). *Summer of the mariposas*. New York, NY: Tu Books. A novel that brings together Greek and Mexican mythology in celebration of the Mexican American culture.

Tran, G. B. (2010). *Vietnamerica: A family's journey*. New York, NY: Villard Books. A graphic novel that explores the experience of returning to a parents' homeland and passing the American dream on to one's children.

Gallo, D. R. (Ed.). (2004). *First crossing: Stories about teen immigrants*. Cambridge, MA: Candlewick Press. A short story anthology that looks at experiences of fitting in, learning a new language, and experiencing a new culture from many different viewpoints.

Park, L. S. (2010). *A long walk to water: Based on a true story*. New York, NY: Houghton Mifflin Harcourt. A short middle grade novel about the lost boys of Sudan, life in a village, and the life-changing event of receiving a well in another country.

Wilson, T. (2016). *Through my eyes.* Edina, MN: Beaver's Pond Press. An easy-to-read chapter book on the refugee experience, being proud of being Muslim, and adjusting to a new culture.

Khan, M. (2011). *The hijab boutique.* Leicestershire, UK: The Islam Foundation. A novel for young readers about the experience of wearing a hijab and parents starting a business.

embedded experiences, which might also be beneficial for your students. You can locate additional texts that position particular students as experts as you learn more about them.

How-To Essays

As you learn about students' experiences through your reading, encourage them to share their lived experiences orally and in writing. Sharing through spoken language in class discussions or partner talk is a good starting place, but students also need practice and instruction on writing essays, which can be daunting in a second language. One writing task that leverages their lived experiences is a how-to essay on something they are familiar with doing. I help students identify what they uniquely know how to do. Through a thematic unit on Fitting In and Standing Out, students regularly write about their lived experiences in their journal as guided by our reading. Then, I ask students to choose a journal entry they can expand on that explains something they uniquely know how to do—what makes them stand out. In one class, however, Arun told me he had nothing to write about, so I began looking at picture books with him and asking him questions. When we came to a picture of a bird, he realized that he knew how to do something I did not—how to use a slingshot to kill birds for his family to eat, as he had done as a child in another country. He had to use a lot of detail to explain to me in writing how to make the slingshot and how to use it to successfully slay his family's meal. In order to elicit more detail, I kept asking questions, prompting him to explain to the less experienced teacher what I would need to do to craft a weapon and use it to provide food for my family. Once he had sufficient detail and the order of events correct in his essay, I helped him add transition words and edit for grammar and spelling.

If you engage in this activity with your students, the essays will probably be diverse, as illustrated from these examples. Camille wrote her essay on how to harvest corn in an African village as mentored by an excerpt from *Jambo Means Hello* (Feelings & Feelings, 1974). Hla explained in her essay how *thanakha paste* was made using the bark of a tree after we read a book together, *M Is for Myanmar* (Rush, 2011), and she realized some of us knew nothing about this culturally significant part of her life. She even wore it on her face in intricate designs to class one day to illustrate the final product and explain the many benefits of this paste. (I was told it would make me look younger!). Figure 5.3 provides an excerpt from a student's essay on how to kill and cook a chicken from her experiences, which differed from those of other students. It is interesting that students from different cultures will explain the methods for poultry slaughter and preparation quite differently. This allows the class to see the same practice through various culturally-specific lenses while highlighting their own experiences and developing writing skills.

Narratives

Olson, Scarcella, and Matuchniak (2015) suggest making narrative writing a priority with secondary English learners because this form of writing builds on what students already know—their lived experiences. Through writing about stories from their own lives, students share themselves with the teacher and others, as well as focus on giving rich descriptions and expanding their vocabulary. In order to facilitate this genre of writing, it is important that students are reading various texts that can serve as mentor texts that model how they might write their own stories and signify that their life stories are worthy of being in print (Newman, 2012). As they read texts individually and with the class, have students write down connections they can make between the reading and their personal experiences in their journal. This will give them a wealth of ideas to choose from when it is time for them to begin their narrative.

I often have students write narratives about their own lives, accompanied by their self-created visuals using technology, collages, drawings, or photography. The goal is for them to explain the narrative of their life using a visual to help them convey meaning. They can write about their immigration

Figure 5.3. Excerpt from a How-To Essay by an Intermediate Student

Chickens

I am from Thailand. We use chickens a lot. We use chickens to eat and to help people wake up early. The roosters crow every day before the sun comes up. We make the same rice we eat for the chickens. The roosters also fight so people can make money.

To kill the chicken, sometimes we shot it with a slingshot. We also held its neck with our hands to kill it. Then, we cut out the organs and threw them away. Next, we put it in a pot with oil, salt, a type of lettuce, and a sweet sauce called *a cho mo*.

journeys (see Chapter 4), a time they were the happiest, their first day in U.S. schools, or when they were proud of an accomplishment. Many students might say they do not know what to write about, but you can provide them examples as they respond to texts that reflect their lived experiences. Read "Grandma Was Never Young" in the collection of stories in *Fitting In* (Bernardo, 1996) to encourage students to write about a time when they translated for their family. Maybe they've had some moments in their new culture that were embarrassing but now they can look back on them as humorous. Read the short story "The All-American Slurp" (Namioka, 2003) to encourage them to write about those moments. As you read with students, continually stop and allow them to write about their connections in their journal and then they will have plenty of ideas to choose from to write their personal narratives.

READING BEYOND STUDENTS' EXPERIENCES

Of course we want to make sure that students have many texts that are mirrors (Sims Bishop, 1990)—culturally relevant texts where they see their lived experiences reflected back at them. We want them to read from the Homeplace Position (Brooks & Browne, 2012) to give them special insight and more entry points to make meaning from their reading, increasing their English acquisition. Yet, we also want to be purposeful in providing students with windows in texts, reading that helps them understand other people's life and experiences. We hope these experiences are "sliding glass doors" (Sims Bishop, 1990) where students can step into previously unimagined worlds.

Sometimes our students will encounter window texts that neither they nor we have chosen. Although we must work to diversify the literary canon for all students (Campano & Ghiso, 2011), it still exists in most secondary ELA classrooms (Lewis & Dockter, 2011). Our teaching of this literature can still be rich as we work to give students ways to make meaning with text that might not relate very well to their lives and lived experiences.

But how do we do that? Claudia Haag's experience as an ESL teacher, reading and responding to *Charlotte's Web* (White, 1952) with 4th-grade students (Haag & Compton, 2015), provides crucial insight into that burning question many teachers face. When she was given the task of reading and completing a project on this popular novel with her newcomer students, Haag realized that they became very discouraged when reading the text, partially because of the author's prolific vocabulary choices used to describe the scenes. Furthermore, the students did not have experiences on a farm in the Midwestern United States where the story takes place, and, as a result, some of the academic language about farms within the text created a frustrating experience for students who were unfamiliar with farming. In response, Haag let the students express their frustration openly and share solutions to their problem. The students came up with the idea of watching the movie first, giving Haag an opportunity to build the background knowledge necessary for these language learners to comprehend the text. The students also suggested that Haag interactively read the book aloud to them while they followed along in their own copies—what I term *shared reading*. Finally, for reader response activities, the students completed multimodal projects from the book, further allowing them to make meaningful connections to a text that they initially did not understand (Haag & Compton, 2015).

Using a critical eye to evaluate her own teaching, Claudia Haag acknowledged that the text privileged *her* lived experiences, rather than those of her students. She was only able to recognize this because she had previously invested time in learning about her students' lives and experiences through literacy. By knowing her students and then listening to their voices, she was able to provide the right scaffolding to help them gain literacy and language skills through reading and responding to a book that initially seemed difficult to understand.

It is also notable how she listened to their solutions to this problem, the first being that they watch the movie before reading the book. I have often shown a movie after the class completes a book, such as watching the film *Malcolm X* after reading *By Any Means Necessary* (Myers, 1993). However, learning about Haag's experience has given me new insight that it might be more appropriate to watch a movie first when students need to build a lot of background knowledge. I also want to emphasize how these students, like the adolescents I've worked with, thought shared reading would help them make sense of the text—having the teacher read out loud with pauses for clarification and connections, while students follow along in their own copy of the text.

In the secondary classroom, we certainly want to provide our students with window experiences in literature; then, after they have had multiple experiences seeing their own lived experiences reflected back in text, high-interest novels on other subjects at the appropriate English level can help broaden their thinking. Intermediate-level students might enjoy the I Survived series by Lauren Tarshis (http://isurvived.scholastic.com/books), which consists of short, highly engaging chapter books that describe how the preteen protagonists survived historical world events such as the Nazi invasion or the 9/11 terrorist attacks. The website also contains facts about each of these events that students can further explore. Other books that intermediate- to advanced-level ELs I've worked with have enjoyed include *The Watsons Go to Birmingham* (Curtis, 1995) and *Wonder* (Palacio, 2013), which are informative on colloquial speech and cultural norms within the United States at different time periods. If students need support for these books, they might want to take Claudia Haag's ESL students' advice and watch the movies first to help them make the most meaning from text. Another option is for them to listen to the audiobook while they read along, which will provide aural and visual cues for the text.

Particularly at the high school level, we might sometimes need to teach a specific novel as part of the school's or state's curriculum. Though I highly discourage giving students reading that is far beyond their readiness in English, consider how you can provide the support to bring the book to their instructional reading level and make it relevant to their lives. Listen to your students' voices as you reflect on what you might do to build the background knowledge for them to make meaning from the text. But, most important, ensure that your students—all of your students—have large amounts of accessible reading that will connect to their cultures and leverage their lived experiences.

ACTION TIME

- Think about your own culture. Create a graphic organizer to write down "the Fs" of this culture. Consider how these do or do not adequately represent you. What is left unsaid?

- Complete this same activity with students, using a graphic organizer and sentence stems for them to write and speak about their own culture. Then, have them interview other students about their cultures.

- Employing the resources provided in the tables, find at least one book about every country represented by your students or their family members. Then, look for websites or articles that support those texts.

- Have students create a formal presentation about themselves using technology. Try the following websites to create interesting presentations:
  - ✓ https://www.powtoon.com/
  - ✓ https://prezi.com/
  - ✓ http://www.pechakucha.org/ (Students can use PowerPoint to create a Pecha Kucha, using 20 slides with primarily visuals that run for only 20 seconds each. This can be a fun activity to try to keep up with their slides in a fun and supportive environment that always allows for second and third chances!)

- Guide students in creating their own biographical acrostics. This website (http://www.readwritethink.org/classroom-resources/mobile-apps/acrostic-poems-a-31059.html) allows students to use technology to create their poems.

- Listen to this podcast on Latino Literature for Teens: http://www.readwritethink.org/parent-afterschool-resources/

podcast-episodes/latino-literature-teens-30972.html. How can you help your Latino students connect their cultural experiences to literature? Now, apply this to your other students who are not Latino. How will you connect their experiences to your classroom reading?

- High school English teachers often tell me that the books in their school library are too complex for their beginner or intermediate ELs. Get to know a children's librarian and bring in texts for your students to try. If you teach students who qualify, purchase literature appropriate for them at First Book (firstbook.org) at reduced prices.

CHAPTER 6

Support Biliteracy Development

Sara and Aisha sit at the same table in Marie's sheltered English I class. Sara is an 18-year-old from Colombia who reads very well in her native language. Novels in Spanish are her constant companions and Marie encourages her to read in Spanish for some of the assignments in her more challenging mainstream English III class. Sara not only reads in Spanish to complete academic work and more fully participate in the classroom discussions, but also, she tells me, to escape and relax. She reads widely, choosing books about political events in Colombia, the Holocaust, lovestruck vampires, and dystopian worlds, always telling me what she'd like to read next before she's even finished her current book. Although her English reading is still developing, she can read just about anything she wants in Spanish and discusses these novels with me like a true book critic.

Aisha, a 17-year-old from Uganda whose English abilities are similar to Sara's, has completed two chapter books in English through shared reading with Marie and has finished many picture books independently; however, she cannot read in her first language, Luganda. She never missed a year of school in her country, but she essentially fell through the cracks in classrooms that had many more students than U.S. norms. She tells me with much sincerity, though, that she wants to learn to read in what she calls "my language." Although I do not speak her language, nor does anyone else in the school, I make attempts to support her L1 development with a picture dictionary of single words in Luganda as well as bilingual picture books in English and Luganda that have cultural connections to her country. She is teaching herself to read the individual words in the picture dictionary; however, an alarming conversation with her illustrates that she still needs much support to read in Luganda. After she takes the first bilingual book home for the weekend, I ask her if she enjoyed it, and she smiles, telling me what she liked about the book. When I ask if she could read it in Luganda after she read in English, she becomes confused and I suddenly realize that she did not know the other written language was her language—Luganda. When I explain that to her, she sadly tells me she cannot read any of the Luganda words displayed underneath the English. From that point on, I commit to providing her with more resources to learn reading skills in her L1, recognizing the importance of giving her time during school for this challenge, and speaking to her parents about how they might support her at home because Aisha tells me her parents can read in Luganda.

Both Aisha and Sara represent two very different ends of the spectrum of L1 development, although they are in the same class, reading and discussing some of the same books in English. We should view both of them as more than the EL label denotes. They are bilinguals whose biliteracy development needs to be addressed in their ESL and ELA classrooms, albeit in very different ways, given their different abilities in the L1.

BILTERACY WITHIN MONOLINGUAL STANDARDS

For the purposes of applying bilingual research to our teaching, I want to very simply define bilingualism as the ability to speak in two languages and biliteracy as the ability to read and write in two languages (in addition to listening and speaking) for various purposes (Beeman & Urow, 2013). Thus, we can apply the growing body of research on bilingualism and its effects on one's opportunities throughout life (Callahan & Gándara, 2014) to Sara and Aisha. It is crucial for them not just to speak their languages (Spanish/ English and Luganda/English), but to be able to read and write for social and academic purposes in all of their languages.

Yet, for most of you reading this book, all the standards by which your students (and, by default, you) will be evaluated concern only the students' abilities in English. However, you can still promote your students' biliteracy within monolingual standards; in fact, this is a key issue of social justice for our English learners who *are* bilingual students (García & Kleyn, 2016). Callahan and Gándara's (2014) synthesis of many research studies indicates that there is virtually no economic advantage to mere bilingualism in the modern U.S. economy; that is, people who have the ability to speak and understand two languages do not, on average, earn more than English monolinguals. Thus, there is not an economic gain for Sara or Aisha because they are fluent Spanish and Luganda speakers, respectively, who are on their way to developing English fluency. However, the researchers do note a significant economic advantage over English monolinguals when reading and writing abilities in the two languages are taken into account. We can deduce that Sara, because she is highly literate in Spanish, can experience significant financial advantages if she fully develops her English and maintains her Spanish abilities.

This is because those who possess biliteracy in English and another language are likely to make more money than their monolingual counterparts as well as bilinguals who do not know how to read and write at high levels in both languages (Rumbaut, 2014). These biliterate people are also more likely (as compared to English-speaking monolinguals and limited bilinguals) to graduate from high school (Rumbaut, 2014) and enroll in college, particularly a 4-year university (Santibañez & Zárate, 2014). This new research coincides with earlier work that clearly demonstrates that current and former ELs are more successful on standardized assessments in English taken in school when they have developed their literacy skills in both languages (Collier & Thomas, 2009; Thomas & Collier, 2012).

In short, a growing body of research suggests that biliteracy is our ELs' best card to play as they strive for success in our classrooms and beyond. Their ability to speak in their first language is already an asset, but if we can create an environment, as Marie did, that supports students like Sara to use their L1 abilities for academic success in English, it can be a significant factor for her future. Knowing the power of being biliterate, we must also be purposeful in helping students like Aisha, who want and need to learn to read and write in their L1s, by first acknowledging the benefits that reading and writing in their L1 will afford them. In Aisha's case, we need to talk to her and to her parents, explaining the importance of biliteracy and providing them with basic resources to use at school and home so she can begin to learn to read in her L1. When possible, we should also enlist the help of community organizations or university students who read and write the language that needs to be developed, offering our support through knowledge of the research and how to access resources.

Of course, there are many students who fall in between these two extremes that I've shared through Sara and Aisha's stories. For all our students, we can choose to take the stance that all of their languages matter, and affect both their future trajectory in school and society. Our students are bilinguals who can reap the advantages of these coveted skills that are needed increasingly more in a highly connected world (Suárez-Orozco et al., 2008). If we ignore their L1 development, we essentially take away something that would give them a great advantage for their futures. Even if our standards come from a monolingual perspective, we have an obligation to prepare our students for the world beyond high school, giving them every opportunity for success in the labor market.

Therefore, although it is doubtful that your supervisors, school board, or even state and federal officials will hold you accountable for your students' Korean, Arabic, Hindi, or Spanish literacy, you still have very good reasons to be the champion of their first language development. We have an obligation to ensure that our students are successful. I suggest becoming familiar with the following websites, which regularly share the latest research on the benefits of biliteracy:

- The research section on the Seal of Biliteracy's website: http://sealofbiliteracy.org/research
- Reports from the Californians Together website, focusing on multiple pathways through which students can develop biliteracy, with special attention to long-term ELs: https://www.californianstogether.org/
- The website for the Center for Applied Linguistics, where a search on the word *biliteracy* will return more than 100 research reports

and articles on how schools are supporting biliteracy: http://www.cal.org/

- The report *Recognizing the Economic Advantages of a Multilingual Workforce* (Gándara & Acevdeo, 2016) can be found on the Civil Rights Project website: https://www.civilrightsproject.ucla.edu/research/k-12-education/language-minority-students/realizing-the-economic-advantages-of-a-multilingual-workforce

It is important to have your reasoning prepared for every curricular and instructional choice and to be ready to defend your actions in the classroom, especially if those choices entail supporting the language and literacy development of a non-English language. You will need to explain the benefits of biliteracy directly to your students, but also to their parents, other teachers, your principal, and maybe even your school board.

Because we teach bilingual students, we are bilingual educators, providing the resources for every one of our students to develop advanced language abilities in all of their languages, even when we do not speak those languages ourselves. There, indeed, are many accounts of how middle and high school teachers who do not speak their students' first languages can support their further development in the classroom (Cook, 2001; Cummins, 2007; Ebe & Chapman-Santiago, 2016; García, Flores, & Chu, 2011; García et al., 2017; García & Sylvan, 2011).

AFFIRMING STUDENTS' LANGUAGES

Supporting biliteracy development begins with the *affirm* component in R.E.A.L. instruction. In previous chapters, we considered how to affirm students' cultures and lived experiences. R.E.A.L. instruction should also affirm ELs' multiple languages and their language abilities (Cummins, et al., 2005). Because English learners are not monolingual students, we should not teach them as if they were, pretending like their L1s do not exist in the English classroom. They are bilinguals who already possess oral language skills and perhaps even reading and writing abilities in at least one language other than English (Menken, 2013)—strengths the ESL and ELA teacher can capitalize on and continue to develop.

Learn About Students' Language Abilities

First, we must learn about students' language/s, their abilities in each language, and for what purposes they use their languages (García et al., 2017). We also need to recognize that ELs might orally translate for their family on a regular basis. This is referred to as language brokering (Tse, 1996) and is a very common activity engaged in by immigrant youth that provides a great resource not just to their families but to all of society (Orellana, 2009). Language brokering usually goes unnoticed at school, but we can be purposeful in acknowledging students' skills and encourage them to continue to sharpen their language brokering because it can be a great benefit for their futures. They might use their translation skills for employment purposes or to serve others in their communities. Nurturing this ability can help students become more aware of the special skills they possess within the academic classroom.

For example, I worked with a student who had not passed many of his classes and was considered a long-term EL, investigating how his experiences in school compared with his out-of-school life and literacies in order to understand how we might support him more in the high school classroom. His oral English was as fluent as mine, and he even read chapter books written for adults in English. Although his language brokering abilities were amazing, they went unnoticed at school as he struggled through his classes. His teachers were unaware of the language brokering he performed on a regular basis, and particularly the fact that he translated the sermons at his church from English to Spanish through a live broadcast. He also told me that when he sometimes spent the night in jail for panhandling, he exercised this skill. He laughed about how he was often asked to translate for some of the other "clients" who needed to communicate with police officers. In fact, he translated so frequently in his life outside of school that he joked, "I'm the translator for the world!"

Another student who was a recent arrival to the United States explained to me that at family meals, he used a mixture of English, Lingala, and French, depending on whom he was speaking to and what he wanted to communicate. A simple family meal required him to think about which language to use for specific purposes with different people—an exercise in critical thinking. Our English learners will also use language in advanced ways that we might not be aware of because our life experiences differ. There is a wealth of knowledge for us to discover just about this one area in our students' lives; thus, we need to learn about students' language use outside of school so we can acknowledge their skills and utilize them to further students' academic achievement. By taking the time to learn about what is usually ignored, we affirm our students as multilinguals who use language in advanced and diverse ways.

Learn Phrases in Students' Languages

Second, in order to affirm students' multiple languages, we should try to learn at least a few words or phrases in each of those languages. Some teachers keep "cheat sheets" on their desk of greetings such as "good morning" spelled phonetically using the English alphabet and sounds. As each student enters your classroom, you can affirm him or her with your greeting, setting the tone for the rest of the class. All teachers should make the effort to be a language learner with students and to seek their guidance to learn the correct pronunciation and meaning of phrases. You can have students label posters or charts in the room with words in their language, which will also give them a visual representation that you acknowledge their skills in another language.

Marco, an EL in the 10th grade, tells me about his first year in the United States as a 7th-grader. He had a very positive experience and I ask him what contributed to that. With a smile, he eagerly tells me about his ESL teacher who tried to speak to him in Spanish. She knew very little of his language, but he greatly appreciated her efforts and says it made him feel better about mispronouncing words in English. He says one of the best things teachers can do to help students learning English is to try to speak students' languages.

When we become language learners, we can help our ELs see us in a different light. One day, Aye Cho Htay brought to class *la phet tote*, a common dish from Myanmar that she and other students had written about in their journals after we read a book that mentioned the food. She cooked it the night before and brought enough to share with me and the whole class. I wanted to demonstrate my gratitude so I looked up how to say *thank you* in Karen, her language. The next morning as we were beginning, I spoke to the whole class, using my new Karen phrase to show my appreciation for Aye Cho Htay's kind act. As I finished my short production, she bowed her head and quietly told me, "You're welcome" in English. I noticed that two other girls began to giggle. The whole class looked at them, not understanding what was funny. Finally, one of the girls blurted out: "Miss, you call Aye Cho Htay crazy!" Then, all three Karen girls could no longer contain their laughter and the rest of the class caught on to my slip-up. The words for "thank you" and "crazy" in Karen sound very similar (to me) and the tones in my pronunciation were just a little off. This became a running joke in the class; we often liked to say something was crazy in Karen. It turned out to be a perfect teachable moment: The students saw me making a genuine language mistake as I took risks, and whenever they had trouble in English, we would recall that moment.

PURPOSEFULLY LEVERAGING THE L1

In addition to acknowledging and affirming students' languages, we need to leverage their full linguistic repertoires for their academic achievement. Based on theories of bilingualism that show the connections among all of one's languages (Cummins, 1979; García & Li Wei, 2014), there are many ways to systematically use students' L1 within the ESL and ELA classroom. However, using students' L1s should not be haphazard; rather, it should be methodically guided by the purpose behind a learning activity to effectively support students' English language and first language literacy development.

L1 as a Support for L2 Development

Many teachers of secondary students have used students' first languages to engage them in English development, strengthen literacy skills that can transfer to any language, provide scaffolding for content learning in English, create identity texts, and engage in higher-order thinking (Cook, 2001; Cummins, 2007; García et al., 2017; Goodwin & Jiménez, 2015). To really walk in your students' shoes, try learning secondary content in a language in which you do not possess grade-level literacy skills. Would support in your L1 be helpful in understanding the language and content? In graduate courses, I have teachers spend at least 10 hours engaged in second language acquisition to help them better understand their students' experiences. Most of them tell me they used oral and written English to help them make sense of the L2 they were learning.

Indeed, if used systemically and appropriately, students' first languages can become a support to their English language development. In fact, to forbid students from using their L1 is like putting them in a straitjacket for their second language acquisition. Their first language is their greatest resource, and we should understand the role it can play in furthering their English and academic skills.

There are various ways an L1 can be used in an English-medium classroom for the primary purpose of English development. Indeed, in the book *The Translanguaging Classroom* (García et al., 2017), which relates how the L1 is used alongside English in three different teachers' instruction, two of the three focal teachers are in English-medium classrooms in secondary schools and do not speak the first languages of the majority of their students. Nevertheless, their classrooms suggest that using the L1 is effective for L2 success. Their students summarize content they are learning in English in the L1, use side-by-side English and L1 versions of text, and demonstrate their learning by creating products in two languages. The reason these activities are successful coincides with bilingual and second language acquisition theories—namely, seeing all of one's languages as part of a full linguistic repertoire (García & Kleyn, 2016) as well as understanding the need for comprehensible input in order for second language acquisition to occur (Krashen, 1994).

To illustrate, consider the following: Language learners need comprehensible input through what they read, see, and hear—their receptive language (Krashen, 1994; Ortega, 2009). Being able to pause and clarify one's understanding of a text or video by talking to a partner in the L1 can be very beneficial to their meaning-making from the text and can also serve to clarify any misunderstood information.

The L1 can also be used to help students understand content that is above their reading level in English and to allow them a way to participate in response activities in English. Content learned in one language does not need to be relearned in another because students just need vocabulary to express that content in another language (Baker, 2011). For example, students might be discussing a novel in English that is too complex because of its vocabulary, syntactical structures, or Lexile level for them to comprehend. I was reading *Dying to Cross: The Worst Tragedy in Immigrant History* (Ramos, 2005) with a small, multileveled literature response group of ELs in Kelly's classroom. Two of the students could not make much meaning from the text, which caused frustration, difficulty completing writing assignments such as graphic organizers, and disengagement in our small-group discussion. However, after I gave them the Spanish version of the novel (Ramos, 2005), which is actually the original language of the text, they understood the story because they had grade-level reading abilities in Spanish. I provided them with keywords in English and they were able to complete the writing assignments and participate in the discussions in English with the rest of their small group. They participated in meaningful activities in the L2, furthering their second language acquisition, because they were able to read the content in their L1.

Sometimes students will want to read a novel first in their L1 before they read it in English. This helps them make more meaning from the English text. Paula, a newcomer from Mexico, was trying to read the young adult novel *Finding Miracles* (Álvarez, 2006b) independently. She was having a lot of difficulty understanding the English, so she asked for the book in Spanish, *En Busca de Milagros* (Álvarez, 2006a). After reading the book in Spanish with ease, she was able to return to the English version and finish it with more comprehension. She completed double the amount of reading, but through her use of the L1, she could finish her first novel in English—an accomplishment that gave her a lot of pride.

Another way of using the L1 for L2 support is to understand specific vocabulary. When learning vocabulary around a theme, students can write the more abstract words in their journals with a translation into their first language. Considering the many new words that ELs will encounter in your class and in other subjects on a daily basis, they can benefit from having a quick translation of particular vocabulary that reoccurs within a theme. It can also be very beneficial to add these words in many languages to your word wall where you display new words in a theme. Figure 6.1 shows how a student from China kept a list of the main vocabulary from the theme in his ELA class in Chinese so he could reference it regularly for quick comprehension.

Sanctioning a Space for Translanguaging

There are many other reasons to use the L1 that extend beyond L2 acquisition. If we really want to affirm our students and acknowledge them for who they are through an asset-oriented perspective, then we must purposefully provide a space for them to express their bilingual identities in the classroom (Cummins et al., 2005). Translanguaging, or drawing upon one's full

Figure 6.1. Student's Journal in English and Chinese

隔离 · Segregation – Separate what you don't like
区别 · Discrimination – to treat people differently
分离 · Separate – different
公平 · Fair – right (good) for everyone
平等 · Equality – same opportunities

linguistic repertoire, allows students to entirely utilize all their language resources to accomplish a goal (García & Li Wei, 2014). Most of our ELs are translanguaging in our English-medium classrooms, whether we recognize it or not. Daniel and Pacheco (2016) explain that multilingual students in their study regularly translanguaged in their English classrooms by using their L1 to take notes about a text they were reading in English, study for tests, clarify assignments, consult a bilingual dictionary, and create writing drafts. Therefore, translanguaging is an exercise we should encourage at particular and purposeful times in our instruction, even going so far as to sanction a space for this practice in the ESL or ELA classroom (Stewart & Hansen-Thomas, 2016), sending the message to students that drawing from all of their languages is advantageous in an official academic space. Encouraging translanguaging provides students with natural spaces for developing higher-order skills such as creativity and critical thinking (García & Li Wei, 2014).

Stewart and Hansen-Thomas (2016) share an example from the high school English classroom relevant to this idea as Paula, an intermediate-level EL wrote a "Where I'm From" poem (Lyon, 1999) in English, then translated her poem into Spanish, and finally, wrote a third poem (shown in Figure 6.2) that creatively intermixed her two languages. Translating her poem from English to Spanish required her to think deeply about language and the nuanced meanings of many words. However, Paula's third poem shows the skills she has available to her that a monolingual student does not. In mixing her languages together in creative writing, she exhibited critical thinking by weighing her options for each phrase, word, or morpheme. What would a Spanish word communicate as compared to an English word? Which one conveyed the meaning she wanted to share? Her bilingualism provides her with many choices, allowing her to engage in high degrees of creativity and critical thinking (García & Li Wei, 2014) we want to tap into and nurture in our students.

Yet, if we want students to write with such innovation, we need to be certain that we provide them with mentor texts in their reading—texts where

Figure 6.2. Excerpt of Student's Translanguaged Poetry

I'm from Eagle Pass, de Morales Piedra,
del pozole and the frijoles borrachos
from the "Man of the Orquestra", the trumpet and the piano,
the weddings and las fotos familiares,
orgullosamente from Melchor Mezquiz, Coahuila.
The famous place where yo creci, del "Martha's", de la "Cascada"
and the family love every single day of my whole life.

they can see the written word portrayed in ways that have often been shunned at school. It is important to note that Paula had the idea to write this third highly creative poem after reading similar poetry such as "Bilingual Love Poem" (Burciaga, 2005). Her translanguaged reading provided her with a mentor text that showed her how she could intertwine her two languages for a poetic expression of her transnational life.

MULTILINGUAL TEXTS

Multilingual texts like the poetry that influenced Paula might creatively weave multiple languages together, but there are many other kinds of texts that you can intentionally use with students as you consider the purpose of a particular reading and the students' L1 reading abilities. Table 6.1 lists different kinds of multilingual texts in some of the languages most commonly spoken at home by English learners in U.S. schools: Spanish, Arabic, Chinese, Vietnamese, Hmong, Haitian/Haitian Creole, and Korean (U.S. Department of Education, 2016). You should ensure that you have literature available to your students for every language represented in your classroom, understanding students' L1 reading level and choosing literature appropriately.

Phrases for Authenticity in English-Medium Books

There are many books written primarily in English that include particular phrases or words in another language, such as *Chu Ju's House* (Whelan, 2004) and *Enchanted Air: Two Cultures, Two Wings: A Memoir* (Engle, 2015), which contain Chinese and Spanish, respectively. The use of these non-English words adds authenticity to the reading and pushes the reader to use many different cues to understand the meaning of the words. Even if we do not know that language, we can often understand the meaning within context, though speakers of that language will understand even more deeply, providing them with special access points to the text. As you are reading a text together as a class through shared reading, those phrases can also provide a space for an EL who speaks that language to become an expert as he or she explains the meaning of the phrase or word to you and the

Table 6.1. Suggested Multilingual Books for Adolescent ELs Based on the Most Common Languages Spoken at Home by ELs in U.S. Public Schools

L1 Phrases in English-Medium Book	Bilingual Books	L1 Texts
Nye, N. S. (2014). *The turtle of Oman: A novel.* New York, NY: Greenwillow Books. English with Arabic words Novel	Engle, M. (2008). *The surrender tree: Poems of Cuba's struggle for freedom* (Bilingual ed.). New York, NY: Henry Holt and Co. Spanish/English Novel in verse	Ada, A. F., & Campoy, F. I. (2013). *¡Sí! Somos Latinos.* Doral, FL: Santillana. Spanish Expository text and poetry
Nye, N. S. (1997). *Habibi.* New York, NY: Simon & Schuster Books for Young Readers. English with Arabic words Novel	Smith, I. (2001). *The lonely queue: The forgotten history of the courageous Chinese Americans in Los Angeles.* Manhattan Beach, CA: East West Discovery Press. Chinese/English Expository text	Stamaty, A. M. (2005). *Muhimat Al Sayyda Alia: Inkaz Kuttub Al Iraq— Alia's mission: Saving the books of Iraq* (Arabic ed.). New York, NY: Alfred A. Knopf. Arabic Graphic novel
Jiménez, J. (2016). *Bloodline.* Houston, TX: Piñata Books, an imprint of Arte Público Press. English with Spanish words Novel	Gerdner, L. (2015). *Grandfather's story cloth.* Manhattan Beach, CA: East West Discovery Press. Hmong/English Picture book	Winter, J. (2002). *Béisbol: Pioneros y leyendas del béisbol latino.* New York, NY: Lee & Low Books. Spanish Expository text
Shea, P. D. (2003). *Tangled threads: A Hmong girl's story.* New York, NY: Clarion Books. English with Hmong words Novel	Ruurs, M. (2016). *Stepping stones: A refugee family's journey* (Trans. F. Raheem). British Columbia, Canada: Orca Book Publishers. Arabic/English Picture book	Johng-Nishikawa, J. (2011). *Dreaming in English: A memoir* (Korean ed.). Davis, CA: Yellow Tree. Korean Memoir

Table 6.1. Suggested Multilingual Books for Adolescent ELs Based on the Most Common Languages Spoken at Home by ELs in U.S. Public Schools (continued)

Smith, I., & Kindert, J. C. (2013). *Three years and eight months*. Manhattan Beach, CA: East West Discovery Press. English with Chinese words Picture book	Tran, T., & Phong, A. (2003). *Going home, coming home*. San Francisco, CA: Children's Book Press. Vietnamese/English Picture book	Jiménez, F. (2000). *Cajas de cartón: Relatos de la vida peregrina de un niño campesino*. Boston, MA: Cengage Learning. Spanish Autobiographical novel
Danticat, E. (2002). *Behind the mountains*. New York, NY: Scholastic. English with Haitian words Novel	Hayes, J. (2004). *Ghost fever*. El Paso, TX: Cinco Puntos Press. Spanish/English Novel	Jiménez, F. (2002). *Senderos fronterizos: Continuación de cajas de cartón*. Boston, MA: Houghton Mifflin. Spanish Autobiographical novel
McCall, G. G. (2016). *Shame the stars*. New York, NY: Tu Books. English with Spanish words Novel	Cha, D., Cha, C., Cha, N. T., & Minnesota Humanities Commission. (2002). *Dia's story cloth*. (Bilingual ed.). St. Paul, MN: Minnesota Humanities Commission. Hmong/English Picture book	Jiménez, F. (2009). *Más allá de mí: Continuación de cajas de cartón y senderos fronterizos*. Boston, MA: Houghton Mifflin. Spanish Autobiographical novel

classmates. An engaging activity that promotes students' skills in using context clues involves first asking the rest of the class to write what they think the non-English word or phrase means, citing evidence for their reasoning. Then, the student who speaks that language can confirm, deny, or expand on each estimation.

Bilingual Books

Some teachers in bilingual programs prefer not to assign bilingual books because students often choose to read in their strongest language and ignore the other one—diminishing the opportunity to develop both languages, which is the purpose of their program and what we want for our ELs as well. Although I understand this problem, bilingual books can be utilized in special ways with adolescents in English-medium classrooms. For example, you might use these books to encourage students to read first in their L1, and then in English, using visuals for support if they are available. More advanced students can read first in English, looking at the L1 only to clarify meaning, and then in their language. You can also use bilingual texts for shared reading by reading the English to the whole class while L1 support is there for students in a multileveled class who need more pathways to comprehension.

For instance, I was teaching about proverbs in one class at the end of the school year in May. Vu was a Vietnamese student who had just arrived in the United States at the beginning of May. The other students were all Spanish-speakers who had all begun the school year that August, and some were even in their second year in U.S. schools. Needless to say, the English reading level among these students was vast. We read together from a bilingual English/Vietnamese book that contains Vietnamese proverbs. Although Vu understood very little English, he could read the Vietnamese, allowing for us to engage in reading and responding to a shared text together despite large language barriers. Certainly, showing up for your first day in a U.S. high school in May is not ideal, but through the use of this text, I hope we were able to welcome Vu and provide him with access to English acquisition and course content, while still engaging in end-of-year activities that furthered the learning of the other students.

L1 Texts for Independent Reading

What I want most for students is for them to read and develop a love of reading that will extend throughout their lifetimes. I want them to learn about the world, make sense of their own experiences, discover new possibilities, and even escape when needed through literature. As they do that, I know they are gaining knowledge, new perspectives, and coping skills, along with literacy abilities. If your students can read in their first language, they should not have to wait years before they can engage in the reading that would be most meaningful to them because they cannot yet read a novel in English. They should be reading self-selected and interesting texts at their independent reading level all the time. Because it takes years to acquire advanced literacy skills in another language (Baker, 2011), you need to ensure that they have access to L1 books long before they have the skills to read the same book in English.

When students realize I will do my best to find them something they want to read, requests come in even from those who might seem like reluctant readers, who often request the newest young adult novel-turned-movie in their language. Some students request really advanced texts in their L1s while others enjoy taking L1 picture books home to read "with their little brother or sister," although I suspect many of them are reading these for their own enjoyment as well. Regardless of students' reading levels in the L1, we need to ensure that they have appropriate L1 literature to read both in class and at home. Two publishers that offer many children's, adolescent, and young adult literature in languages other than English are Lectorum, which publishes in Spanish, and East West Discovery Press, which publishes in many languages, including Arabic, Chinese, Vietnamese, Hmong, and Spanish.

MULTILINGUAL RESPONSES

Students' multilingual reading will provide them with mentor texts for multilingual or L1 responses to their reading. Sometimes they might not have considered how they can use their L1 in writing until they have seen examples of translanguaged writing, literature that includes more than one language, in your classroom (Pérez Rosario, 2014). A steady diet of writing and speaking (productive language) in their various L1s is beneficial even if you do not understand those languages yourself. When students are talking or writing in Arabic, I do not understand it, but I know it is crucial for them to do this in order to develop their biliteracy. I strongly encourage students to respond to their reading in all their languages, even those I do not know, and sometimes having another student translate when possible.

Writing in All Languages

All students, but particularly ELs, need to write regularly for different purposes, and that writing should include all of their languages. I often encourage students to write to learn—that is, to make meaning from the text during pauses in our reading. Sometimes I ask them to write in the L1, especially if that helps them better understand their reading. I also encourage students to engage in sustained journal writing in their L1s to become accustomed to putting their thoughts or feelings on the page and to develop the stamina of writing for longer periods of time.

It is important to give students authentic reasons to write in both languages, understanding that they have more influence or power if they can communicate their message to readers of more than one language. Involve them in writing letters to the editor in both L1 and English-medium newspapers. Or, if they write a poem or essay they are very proud of, have them publish it in both of their languages so more people can read it. Figure 6.3 illustrates a student's poster that included her poetry about herself in English and Arabic. Even though her teacher did not know Arabic, she encouraged the student to share poetry written in all of her languages through a display in the school. This sent the student the message that she was seen and valued

Figure 6.3. Student's Poetry in English and Arabic (Top Left) Accompanies a Poster About Her Palestinian and Jordanian Heritage

The poster is cropped not to show the artistic display of the student's name that she wrote with an acrostic poem that extended down the right side of her poster.

as a bilingual within her high school. All ELs need to realize that biliteracy skills can be very advantageous for their futures (Callahan & Gándara, 2014), providing them more opportunities to advance their careers and contribute to their society.

Translating Short Passages of Text

As mentioned previously, most ELs engage in translating or language brokering on a regular basis. You can further develop this skill within the classroom to build on students' current literacy practices. Goodwin and Jiménez (2015) advocate for the TRANSLATE method, which groups students who speak the same L1 together to collaborate on a translation. Groups read an academic text, translate a key passage in collaborative L1 groups, and then evaluate these translations. Students who have had difficulty understanding the passage must analyze it closely with their peers in order to translate it. They also develop metacognitive awareness by discussing the differences between English and their L1 to understand what makes an effective translation. Indeed, research (Jiménez et al., 2015) with 50 bilingual students in grades 2 through 8 shows that students improve their metalinguistic awareness when engaging in collaborative translation—they increase their ability to understand the structural components and functions of their languages, leading to greater reading comprehension. The researchers (Goodwin & Jiménez, 2015; Jiménez et al., 2015) note that the TRANSLATE method is not just for bilingual teachers. Any teacher, even if he or she does not speak the students' language, can use this strategy in the classroom to support student learning.

Inserting Authentic Language in Narratives or Scripts

Beginning and intermediate-level ELs often benefit from writing in English by composing their own narratives based on their lives (Olson et al., 2015). It is natural that some of the nouns and dialogue in these personal narratives might best be communicated in students' L1. As you provide students with mentor texts that show how other authors write from their lived experiences using purposeful insertions of the L1 (see Table 6.1), students will be able to do this independently. They need to use enough English to provide context for the reader to understand their meaning, even if he or she does not know the students' L1. Providing the right amount of context and determining when to use the L1 is a writing skill students will develop as they engage in narrative writing from their own lives.

L1 Book Clubs

We want our students to love reading and to do it voluntarily out of class. After-school or lunchtime book clubs can engage students in self-selected and sustained L1 reading. There are many benefits to book clubs—notably, the community of readers that develops. If you have enough students who speak a common L1, group them together to read a text they select. You might support them by providing a list of questions they can use to discuss the text if they need assistance. However, let the students themselves take ownership of these groups and remind them that you are there to offer help, but they have control over what they read and how they respond to it.

In order to really be a champion for ELs at your school, take an extra step toward positioning them in places of prominence among their peers if they are willing and ready. Through partnering with the world language teachers, locate non-ELs in the school who are taking advanced language classes and want to further their skills through book clubs using Spanish, French, and other languages spoken by ELs in your school. This will help ELs develop relationships with other students and will facilitate their opportunity to emerge as the leaders, the language experts. Furthermore, this act will encourage all students and faculty to view ELs' linguistic resources as a benefit to the entire school.

ACTION TIME

- Watch the YouTube video of Dr. Patricia Gándara explaining the benefits of biliteracy not only for our bilingual students but for the entire economy (available at https://www.youtube.com/watch?v=j4jWMuX7INY&index=3&list=PLLigJtUGHmepkSX-EQqOnONDF935Krb5BY&t=2835s).

- Show the video to your students and have them develop material in multiple languages for their parents and other students that explains why they need to develop reading and writing skills in both English and their first language.

- Ask other teachers and the principal for ways students' abilities can be highlighted in the school by translating posters, announcements, or flyers. Inquire about how your ELs can showcase their L2 abilities by providing multilingual announcements or introduction of guest speakers.

- Ensure that you have books that fit into each of the three L1 categories (English books with L1 words, bilingual books, and L1 books) in all of your students' L1s. Enlist their Internet searching skills to help you locate hard copies and electronic versions of texts in their language.

- Find out more about translanguaging in the academic setting by reading the translanguaging guide from the CUNY-NYS Initiative on Emergent Bilinguals (available at http://www.cuny-nysieb.org/translanguaging-resources/translanguaging-guides/).

- Help your students create their own bilingual poetry using this lesson: http://www.readwritethink.org/classroom-resources/lesson-plans/crossing-boundaries-through-bilingual-30525.html

Keep It R.E.A.L.—Play to Win!

Karmen is a former English learner who, despite a rocky path through high school, is now 26 years old and pursuing a college degree in bilingual education. I take her with me to a conference presentation about the power of culturally relevant texts and ask her to choose a poem from an anthology to read aloud and explain to a group of teachers why it resonates with her. She chooses "Why Am I So Brown?" (Sánchez, 1994), a poem that weaves together both English and Spanish. In the middle of my presentation, I invite her to the front to read the poem aloud. She begins with confidence, reading boldly, but soon tears well up and her voice is shaking. She looks over at me and I nod my encouragement for her to continue. As she finishes the last section, "Finally, mi'ja, God made you brown, because it is one of HER favorite colors!" (p. 99), she is too overwhelmed with emotion to speak anymore, but it doesn't matter. Everyone erupts in applause while wiping their own tears.

She keeps it real.

Karmen does not need to tell us why we should use this poem or other culturally relevant texts in the classroom—her visibly emotional transaction with the author, Trinidad Sánchez, Jr., provides the reason. In fact, her 2-minute read-aloud communicated more to those teachers than the other 58 minutes of my presentation. I'm overwhelmingly glad I brought her along.

Then, later on, Karmen approaches me and says something I will never forget. Still through tears, she looks me in the eye and asks: "Dr. Stewart, why didn't I read anything like that in high school?"

The answer is complex and simple at the same time. It is complex, knowing that her teachers might not have known about the diverse literature available to include in their classrooms, and even if they did, they were probably limited in their curricular choices by high-stakes testing, standardized curriculum, and the pressing need for students like Karmen to improve their academic English.

Yet, the answer is also quite simple: Karmen never read anything like that in high school because she never had access to those texts while she was developing her English language skills—books, poems, and stories she would never forget and that might facilitate other transformative experiences with literacy.

As Karmen reminds us, literacy is powerful—it is how we know and are known to others, how we make sense of the human experience. R.E.A.L.

instruction was born out of a powerful summer of literacy learning that changed me, giving me more insight into life. Thirteen-year-old Lay Su Aung wrote me a letter at the end of that summer, the last part of it shown in Figure C.1. Even though she writes, "You teach from the heart not from the book," one could argue that all I did was teach from books. In fact, I had full autonomy over the curriculum, so we just read literature and responded all summer long—reading, writing, listening, speaking, viewing, and representing in creative ways. However, what she seemed to pick up on was that my heart was in everything we did—every book, poem, writing assignment, and presentation. I loved our reading and reader response activities because they facilitated the development of a community of people who were all participating in the human experience. Perhaps my Simple Rule #5—"I care about you, you care about others (and maybe me, too)"—transformed into something stronger—maybe even love.

For me, teaching from the heart is certainly about relevant, engaging, and affirming literacy with adolescent English learners—the bilingual students in our classes whose promise is great. We keep it real for them because their success is our win—when they make meaningful connections to texts, finish an entire book, critically evaluate issues of social justice, work hard at revising an essay, publish their poetry, act on the agency that their bilingualism and biliteracy provides them, and become leaders in our society.

They are why we keep it real. May we play to win.

Figure C.1. Student Note to Teacher

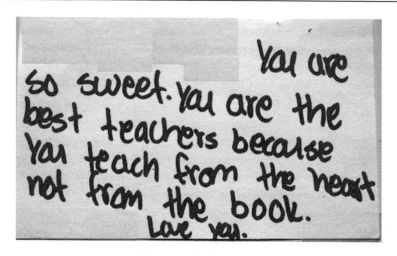

You are so sweet. you are the best teachers because you teach from the heart not from the book. love you.

This is the last of six index cards that the student stapled together to write this note.

Glossary

Academic language: The terminology and sentence structure used in academic settings such as school

Acculturation: Maintaining ties to one's own culture and those cultural practices while understanding and adopting practices of the new culture as well

Asset-oriented stance: Choosing to see students' strengths, rather than focusing on what they lack

Assimilation: Lessening the engagement in one's cultural practices in order to take on those of the new culture

Biliteracy: The ability to read and write, among other literacy skills, in at least two languages

Close reading: Focusing intensely on a text by sustained analysis

Communicative competence: The ability to express an idea and be understood and to be able to understand what others are communicating through language

Comprehensible input: The ability to understand what one sees, reads, and/or hears

Culturally relevant text: A piece of literature that relates to one's cultural experiences, practices, or traditions

Deep culture: The less observable elements of culture, such as the attitudes, values, and beliefs one adopts by belonging to a particular cultural group

Emergent bilingual: A term for students in the process of acquiring English as an additional language that sees the students for their strengths—namely, their bilingualism

English as Second Language (ESL): A class devoted to providing targeted English language instruction to students who are learning English as an additional language

English Language Arts (ELA): A class for all students (ELs and non-ELs) that focuses on developing reading, writing, listening, and speaking skills in English

English learners (ELs): Students who speak a language other than English as their first or primary language and are in the process of acquiring skills in the English language to demonstrate grade-level proficiency as measured by academic assessments

English-medium classroom: A classroom where the teacher provides the primary curriculum and instruction in English and the students will be assessed in English on their learning

Free voluntary reading: Students choose any text they want and choose to read it on their own accord

Guided reading: Reading where the teacher and student both have a copy of the text and the teacher asks the student to read the text with guidance to focus on a particular area (for the purposes of this book, the adolescent students are primarily reading silently during guided reading)

Homeplace Position: According to Brooks & Browne (2012), the cultural place from which readers make meaning from a text based on their ethnicity, culture, religion, and life experiences

i + 1: According to Krashen (1994), the designated place where second language acquisition can best occur, where the input occurs at a level slightly beyond the individual's knowledge of the second language but is comprehensible through context, visuals, or other means

Independent reading: Students read independently without the assistance of the teacher

Inquiry-based learning: Instruction where students deeply investigate questions, problems, or scenarios

L1: The first language, also referred to as the home language

L2: The language students are acquiring, such as English, even if the student already speaks two other languages; English is considered the L2 for English learners

Language code: The rules that govern our use of oral and written language

Language domains: Reading, writing, listening, and speaking

Literacy: The ability to send and receive meaning—more specifically, reading, writing, listening, speaking, viewing, and representing

Long-term English learners (LTELs): Students who have received language support services for 5 or more years and have not yet demonstrated proficiency in English as measured by assessments

Multilingual awareness pedagogy: Viewing ELs through a multilingual lens, understanding how their languages interact, and supporting them in the development of all their languages as explained by García (2008)

Negotiated interaction: Exchanging communication where the language learner can ask for more support in understanding or where the teacher sees that the learner needs support and modifies the interaction for the goal of comprehension

Newcomer: A student who is new to the country and its school system

People group: People with a shared cultural, linguistic, and ethnic identity

Productive vocabulary: Language one can produce through speaking or writing

Pushed output: Structured speaking and writing in which the learner is required to participate for second language acquisition to occur

Read-aloud: The teacher reads a text out loud to students while they listen; for the purposes of this book, in a read-aloud, the students do not have their own copy of the text; they are listening and perhaps viewing the pictures accompanying the text

Reader response: Any writing, speaking, or artistic activity that students complete in response to reading they will begin to do, are currently reading, or have completed

Receptive vocabulary: Language one can understand through reading or listening

Scaffolding: Systematic and temporary support to help learners complete a task that they could not complete independently

Second language acquisition: Adding literacy skills in a language that one does not consider a first, home, or primary language

Shared reading: The teacher reads out loud fluently while the students follow along in their own copies of the text

Sheltered English: English classes for credit, such as English I or English II, specifically designed for ELs and taught by a teacher who is knowledgeable in second language acquisition strategies

Simple rules: Known or unspoken agreements by participants that guide patterns within a system as explained by Patterson et al. (2013)

Students with Interrupted Formal Education (SIFE): Students who arrive to school having missed a significant amount of formal education when other students their age were in school

Students with Limited or Interrupted Formal Education (SLIFE): The same as SIFE but includes students who have been in a formal education setting for all the years their counterparts were in school but experienced education that was lacking in teacher effectiveness, resources, and/or overall quality

Subtractive schooling: An educational environment that ignores students' home languages and cultures as explained by Valenzuela (1999) in her work

Surface culture: Visible elements of culture that are easily detected, such as food, dress, celebrations, and language

Sustained silent reading: Independent reading that occurs for extended periods of uninterrupted time

Translanguaging: The practice of freely moving back and forth between one's full linguistic system; drawing from all of one's languages (García & Li Wei, 2014)

APPENDICES

APPENDIX A: SAMPLE TEXTS FOR
SHORT-TERM UNIT ON ROSA PARKS

Adler, D. A., & Casilla, R. (1993). *A picture book of Rosa Parks.* New York, NY: Holiday House.

Dash, J. (Director), & Qualles, P. (Writer). (2002). *The Rosa Parks story* [TV movie]: Columbia Broadcasting System. Movie that can be used as a culmination to the unit or as a beginning to provide students with background knowledge needed to make meaning from the other texts

Parks, R., & Haskins, J. (1992). *Rosa Parks: My story.* New York, NY: Dial Books. Adolescent novel that can be the focal book of the unit

Parks, R., & Reed, G. J. (1996). *Dear Mrs. Parks: A dialogue with today's youth.* New York, NY: Lee & Low Books. Collection of correspondence between students and Mrs. Parks

Reynolds, A., & Cooper, F. (2009). *Back of the bus.* New York, NY: Philomel Books. Illustrated text to build background knowledge

Rosa Parks Mini-Biography. Available at https://www.youtube.com/watch?v=v8A9gvb5Fh0. YouTube video, less than 5 minutes long, to introduce Rosa Parks to students

What Does It Mean to Stand for Something? Wonderopolis. Available at http://wonderopolis.org/wonder/what-does-it-mean-to-stand-for-something. Article to connect Rosa Parks's legacy to today

Appendix B: Sample World War II Texts and Reader Response Activities

Contribution to Big Idea: World War II	Text for Reading/ Viewing	Genre	Reader Response
Segregation	Sylvia Mendez receiving Medal of Honor from President Obama (available at https://www.youtube.com/watch?v=aXKBSm3sQ2w)	Video	Journal writing: Why do you think Sylvia Mendez is receiving a medal from President Obama?
	Voices of History: Sylvia Mendez by Education Week (available at https://www.youtube.com/watch?v=SIMWdfSxoh8)	Video	Students share what impact Sylvia Mendez has had as partners, followed by group discussion
Segregation	Tonatiuh, D. (2014). *Separate is never equal: Sylvia Mendez & her family's fight for desegregation.* New York, NY: Abrams Books for Young Readers.	Narrative (historical fiction) Illustrated book	Read-aloud Journal writing Class discussion
Segregation	Lewis, J. P. (2012). The child. In J. Corcoran (Ed.), *Dare to dream* (p. 2). Tulsa, OK: Kane Miller Publishing.	Illustrated poetry and informational text	Close reading Journal writing Group discussion
Japanese internment camps	Mochizuki, K., & Lee, D. (1993). *Baseball saved us.* New York, NY: Lee & Low.	Narrative (historical fiction) Illustrated book	Shared reading Journal writing Partner discussion

Appendix B: Sample World War II Texts and Reader Response Activities (cont.)

Contribution to Big Idea: World War II	Reading/Viewing	Genre	Reader Response
Japanese internment camps	Takei, G. (2017). George Takei: Internment, America's great mistake. *New York Times.* Available at https://www.nytimes.com/2017/04/28/opinion/george-takei-japanese-internment-americas-great-mistake.html?_r=0	Newspaper opinion editorial	Close reading
U.S. segregation and Japanese internment camps (Pearl Harbor, atomic bombs, and peace are also mentioned)	Conkling, W. (2011). *Sylvia and Aki.* Berkeley, CA: Tricycle Press.	Narrative (historical fiction) Chapter book	*Focal book Shared and Guided Reading Journal Writing Graphic organizers of characters Edited and published essay
Atomic bombs	Coerr, E., & Himler, R. (1999). *Sadako and the thousand paper cranes.* New York, NY: Puffin.	Narrative (historical fiction) Illustrated book	Read aloud Partner discussion Journal writing
Chinese Americans during World War II and Japanese internment camps	Smith, I. (2008). *Mei Ling in China City.* Manhattan Beach, CA: East West Discovery Press.	Bilingual (English and Chinese) narrative (historical fiction) Illustrated book with informational text	Shared reading Journal writing

Appendix B: Sample World War II Texts and Reader Response Activities (cont.)

Contribution to Big Idea: World War II	Reading/Viewing	Genre	Reader Response
Holocaust	Leyson, L. (2015). *The boy on the wooden box: How the impossible became possible . . . on Schindler's list.* New York, NY: Atheneum Books for Young Readers.	Narrative (memoir) Chapter book	*Focal book Shared reading Journal writing Graphic organizer of plot Timeline of World War II events
Peace	Preus, M., & Takahashi, H. (2008). *The peace bell.* New York, NY: Henry Holt.	Narrative (historical fiction) Illustrated book	Guided reading
All topics related to World War II: Holocaust in Europe, Japanese internment camps, atomic bombs	Atkins, L., & Yogi, S. (2017). *Fred Korematsu speaks up.* Berkeley, CA: Heyday.	Illustrated poetry and informational text	Books available for independent reading. Each student is expected to read at least one of these books during the unit. The teacher helps students select books appropriate for their independent reading levels. (cont'd)
	Leitner, I., & Pedersen, J. (1992). *The big lie: A true story.* New York, NY: Scholastic Inc.	Narrative (biography) Chapter book	
	Boyne, J. (2006). *The boy in the striped pajamas: A fable.* Oxford, England: David Fickling Books.	Narrative (historical fiction) Chapter book	
	Bruchac, J. (2006). *Code talker: A novel about the Navajo marines of World War Two.* New York, NY: Puffin.	Narrative (historical fiction) Young adult novel	
	Fitzmaurice, K. (2012). *A diamond in the desert.* New York, NY: Viking.	Narrative (historical fiction) Chapter book	

Appendix B: Sample World War II Texts and Reader Response Activities (cont.)

Contribution to Big Idea: World War II	Reading/Viewing	Genre	Reader Response
All topics related to World War II: Holocaust in Europe, Japanese internment camps, atomic bombs	Mochizuki, K., & Lee, D. (1997). *Passage to freedom: The Sugihara story.* New York, NY: Lee & Low Books.	Narrative (historical fiction) Illustrated book	(cont'd) Students share their responses to reading through Edmodo while the other students and teachers respond with questions and connections from their books. (cont'd)
	Coerr, E., & Uyehara, H. C. (1993). *Mieko and the fifth treasure.* New York, NY: Putnam.	Narrative (historical fiction) Chapter book	
	Judge, L. (2007). *One thousand tracings: Healing the wounds of World War II.* New York, NY: Hyperion Books for Children.	Narrative (historical fiction) Illustrated book	
	Kramer, A. (2009). *World history biographies: Anne Frank: The young writer who told the world her story.* Washington, DC: National Geographic.	Informational text	
	Lowry, L. (1989). *Number the stars.* Boston, MA: Houghton Mifflin Co.	Narrative (historical fiction) Chapter book	
	Joffo, J., Kris, & Bailly, V. (2013). *A bag of marbles.* Minneapolis, MN: Lerner Publishing.	Graphic novel	
	Nakazawa, K. (1987). *Pies descalzos 1: Una historia de Hiroshima.* New York, NY: Random House.	Graphic novel series in Spanish	

Appendix B: Sample World War II Texts and Reader Response Activities (cont.)

Contribution to Big Idea: World War II	Reading/Viewing	Genre	Reader Response
All topics related to World War II: Holocaust in Europe, Japanese internment camps, atomic bombs	Rubin, S. G. (2011). *Irena Sendler and the children of the Warsaw Ghetto*. New York, NY: Holiday House.	Narrative (biography) Illustrated book	(cont'd) For a culminating activity, students choose one artistic way to represent their book and share it through a presentation (e.g., they could make a poster, collage, playlist, drawing, or other creative project) during the book release party of the anthology of writing published during this unit.
	Ruelle, K. G., & DeSaix, D.D. (2009). *The grand mosque of Paris: A story of how Muslims rescued Jews during the Holocaust*. New York, NY: Holiday House.	Narrative (historical fiction) Illustrated book	
	Moss, M. (2013). *Barbed wire baseball*. New York, NY: Abrams Books for Young Readers.	Narrative (biography) Illustrated book	
	Mochizuki, K., & Lee, D. (1997) *Passage to freedom: The Sugihara story*. New York, NY: Lee & Low.	Narrative (biography) Illustrated book	
	Lee-Tai, M. (2006). *A place where sun flowers grow*. New York, NY: Children's Book Press.	Bilingual (English and Japanese) narrative (historical fiction) Illustrated book	
	Various articles on NewsELA about World War II	Newspaper articles that can be adjusted for text complexity; also available in Spanish	

References

Albright, L. K., & Ariail, M. (2005). Tapping the potential of teacher read-alouds in middle schools. *Journal of Adolescent & Adult Literacy, 48*(7), 582–591.

Araujo, J. (2013). Expanding the learning zone: Decisions that transform the practices of two English language arts teachers. *35th Association of Literacy Educators and Researchers Yearbook* (pp. 87–108). Louisville, KY: Association of Literacy Educators and Researchers.

Araujo, J., & Wickstrom, C. (in press). Writing instruction that makes a difference to English learners. *Acta Universitatis Lodziensis. Folia Librorum,* 1–27.

Atwell, N. (1987). *In the middle: Writing, reading, and learning with adolescents.* Upper Montclair, NJ: Boynton/Cook.

Au, K. H. (1998). Social constructivism and the school literacy learning of students of diverse backgrounds. *Journal of Literacy Research, 30*(2), 297–319.

Au, W. (2011). Teaching under the new Taylorism: High-stakes testing and the standardization of the 21st century curriculum. *Journal of Curriculum Studies, 43*(1), 25–45.

Baker, C. (2011). *Foundations of bilingual education and bilingualism* (5th ed.). Tonawanda, NY: Multilingual Matters.

Beach, R., Appleman, D., Fecho, B., & Simon, R. (2016). *Teaching literature to adolescents* (3rd ed.). New York, NY: Routledge.

Beeman, K., & Urow, C. (2013). *Teaching for biliteracy: Strengthening bridges between languages.* Philadelphia, PA: Caslon, Inc.

Beers, K., & Probst, R. E. (2013). *Notice & note: Strategies for close reading.* Portsmouth, NH: Heinemann.

Bennett, C. I. (2015). *Comprehensive multicultural education: Theory and practice* (8th ed.). Boston, MA: Pearson Education.

Boatright, M. D. (2010). Graphic journeys: Graphic novels' representations of immigrant experiences. *Journal of Adolescent & Adult Literacy, 53*(6), 468–476.

Boyles, N. (2014). *Closer reading grades 3–6.* Thousand Oaks, CA: Corwin.

Brooks, M. D. (2016). How and when did you learn your language? Bilingual students' linguistic experiences and literacy instruction. *Journal of Adolescent & Adult Literacy, 60*(4), 383–393.

Brooks, W. (2006). Reading representations of themselves: Urban youth use culture and African American textual features to develop literary understandings. *Reading Research Quarterly, 41*(3), 372–392.

Brooks, W., & Browne, S. (2012). Towards a culturally situated reader response theory. *Children's Literature in Education, 43*(1), 74–85.

Burkins, J. M., & Croft, M. M. (2010). *Preventing misguided reading: New strategies for guided reading teachers.* Thousand Oaks, CA: Corwin.

Calderón, M. (2007). *Teaching reading to English language learners, grades 6–12: A framework for improving achievement in the content areas.* Thousand Oaks, CA: Corwin.

Calkins, L. (1986). *The art of teaching writing.* Portsmouth, NH: Heinemann.

Callahan, R., & Gándara, P. (2014). *The bilingual advantage: Language, literacy, and the U.S. labor market.* Toronto, Canada: Multilingual Matters.

Campano, G. (2007). *Immigrant students and literacy: Reading, writing, and remembering.* New York, NY: Teachers College Press.

Campano, G., & Ghiso, M. P. (2011). Immigrant students as cosmopolitan individuals. In S. A. Wolf, K. Coats, P. Enciso, & C. A. Jenkins (Eds.), *Handbook of research on children's and young adult literature* (pp. 164–176). New York, NY: Routledge.

Canagarajah, S. (2011). Translanguaging in the classroom: Emerging issues for research and pedagogy. *Applied Linguistics Review, 2,* 1–28.

Cary, S. (2004). *Going graphic: Comics at work in the multilingual classroom.* Portsmouth, NH: Heinemann.

Chappel, S. V., & Faltis, C. (2013). *The arts and emergent bilingual youth: Building culturally responsive, critical and creative education in school and community contexts.* New York, NY: Routledge.

Christensen, L. (2009). *Teaching for joy and justice.* Milwaukee, WI: Rethinking Schools, Ltd.

Chun, C. (2009). Critical literacies and graphic novels for English-language learners: Teaching Maus. *Journal of Adolescent & Adult Literacy 53*(2), 144–153.

Cloud, N., Lakin, J., Leiniger, E., & Maxwell, L. (2010). *Teaching adolescent English language learners: Essential strategies for middle and high school.* Philadelphia, PA: Caslon, Inc.

Collier, V. P. (1995). Acquiring a second language for school. *Directions in Language and Education, 1*(4), 1–8.

Collier, V. P., & Thomas, W. P. (2009). *Educating English learners for a transformed world.* Albuquerque, NM: Dual Language Education of New Mexico/Fuente Press.

Cook, V. (2001). Using the first language in the classroom. *The Canadian Modern Language Review, 57*(3), 402–423.

Culham, R. (2014). *The writing thief: Using mentor texts to teach the craft of writing.* Newark, DE: International Reading Association.

Cummins, J. (1979). Cognitive/academic language proficiency, linguistic interdependence, the optimum age question and some other matters. *Working Papers on Bilingualism, 19,* 198–205.

Cummins, J. (2000). *Language, power, and pedagogy: Bilingual children in the crossfire.* Clevedon, England: Multilingual Matters.

Cummins, J. (2007). Rethinking monolingual instructional strategies in multilingual classrooms. *Canadian Journal of Applied Linguistics/Revue Canadienne de Linguistique, 10*(2), 221–240.

Cummins, J., Bismilla, V., Chow, P., Giampapa, F., Cohen, S., Leoni, L., . . . Sastri, P. (2005). Affirming identity in multilingual classrooms. *Educational Leadership, 63*(1), 38–43.

Daniel, S. M., & Pacheco, M. B. (2016). Translanguaging practices and perspectives of four multilingual teenagers. *Journal of Adolescent & Adult Literacy, 59*(6), 653–663.

Danzak, R. L. (2011). Defining identities through multiliteracies: EL teens narrate their immigration experience as graphic stories. *Journal of Adolescent & Adult Literacy, 55*(3), 187–196.

DeCapua, A., Smathers, W., & Tang, L. F. (2007). Schooling interrupted. *Educational Leadership, 64*(6), 40–46.

Dwyer, B., & Larson, L. (2013). The writer in the reader: Building communities of response in digital environments. In K. E. Pytash & R. E. Ferdig (Eds.), *Exploring technology for writing and writing instruction* (pp. 202–220). Hershey, PA: IGI Global.

Early, M., & Marshall, S. (2008). Adolescent ESL students' interpretation and appreciation of literary texts: A case study of multimodality. *Canadian Modern Language Review/La Revue canadienne des langues vivantes, 64*(3), 377–397.

Ebe, A. E. (2012). Supporting the reading development of middle school English language learners through culturally relevant texts. *Reading & Writing Quarterly, 28*(2), 179–198.

Ebe, A. E., & Chapman-Santiago, C. (2016). Student voices shining through: Exploring translanguaging as a literary device. In O. García & T. Kleyn (Eds.), *Translanguaging with multilingual students: Learning from classroom moments* (pp. 57–82). New York, NY: Routledge.

Echevarría, J., Vogt, M., & Short, D. (2017). *Making content comprehensible for English learners: The SIOP Model* (5th ed.). Boston, MA: Pearson.

Enright, K. A. (2011). Language and literacy for a new mainstream. *American Educational Research Journal, 48*(1), 80–118.

Escamilla, K., Hopewell, S., Butvilofsky, S., Sparrow, W., Soltero-González, L., Ruiz-Figueroa, O., & Escamilla, M. (2014). *Biliteracy from the start: Literacy squared in action*. Philadelphia, PA: Caslon.

Faltis, C., & Coulter, C. (2008). *Teaching English learners and immigrant students in secondary schools*. Upper Saddle River, NJ: Pearson/Merrill Prentice Hall.

Freeman, Y. S., & Freeman, D. E. (2006). *Teaching reading and writing in Spanish and English in bilingual and dual language classrooms* (2nd ed.). Portsmouth, NH: Heinemann.

Freeman, Y. S., Freeman, D. E., & Mercuri, S. (2002). *Closing the achievement gap: How to reach limited-formal-schooling and long-term English learners*. Portsmouth, NH: Heinemann.

Freeman, Y. S., Freeman, D. E., Soto, M., & Ebe, A. (2016). *ESL teaching: Principles for success* (Rev. ed.). Portsmouth: Heinemann.

Freeman, Y. S., Mercuri, S., & Freeman, D. E. (2001). Keys to success for bilingual students with limited formal schooling. *Bilingual Research Journal, 25*, 203–213.

Fu, D. (2009). *Writing between languages: How English language learners make the transition to fluency, grades 4–12.* Portsmouth, NH: Heinemann.

Galda, L., & Graves, M. F. (2007). *Reading and responding in the middle grades: Approaches for all classrooms.* Boston, MA: Pearson Education, Inc.

Gallagher, K. (2009). *Readicide: How schools are killing reading and what you can do about it.* Portland, ME: Stenhouse Publishers.

Gándara, P., & Acevedo, S. (2016). *Realizing the economic advantages of a multilingual workforce.* Available at https://www.civilrightsproject.ucla.edu/research/k-12-education/language-minority-students/realizing-the-economic-advantages-of-a-multilingual-workforce/gandar-acevedo-economic-advantages-bilingual-2016.pdf

García, O. (2008). Multilingual language awareness and teacher education. In J. Cenoz & N. Hornberger (Eds.), *Encyclopedia of language and education vol. 6: Knowledge about language* (2nd ed., pp. 385–400). Berlin, Germany: Springer.

García, O. (2009). *Bilingual education in the 21st century: A global perspective.* Malden, MA: Wiley-Blackwell.

García, O., Flores, N., & Chu, H. (2011). Extending bilingualism in U.S. secondary education: New variations. *International Multilingual Research Journal, 5*(1), 1–18.

García, O., Johnson, S. I., & Seltzer, K. (2017). *The translanguaging classroom: Leveraging student bilingualism for learning.* Philadelphia, PA: Caslon.

García, O., & Kleyn, T. (2016). A translanguaging education policy: Disruptions and creating spaces of possibility. In García & Kleyn (Eds.), *Translanguaging with multilingual students: Learning from classroom moments.* (pp. 181–201). NY: Routledge.

García, O., & Kleifgen, J. A. (2010). *Educating emergent bilinguals: Policies, programs, and practices for English language learners.* New York, NY: Teachers College Press.

García, O., & Sylvan, C. (2011). Pedagogies and practices in multilingual classrooms: Singularities in pluralities. *Modern Language Journal, 95*, 385–400.

García, O., & Wei. L. (2014). *Translanguaging: Language, bilingualism, and education.* New York, NY: Palgrave Pivot.

Garrett, T. (2014). *Effective classroom management: The essentials.* New York, NY: Teachers College Press.

Gee, J. P. (2015). *Social linguistics and literacies: Ideology in discourses* (5th ed.). New York, NY: Routledge, Taylor & Francis Group.

Gibbons, P. (2009). *English learners' academic literacy and thinking: Learning in the challenge zone.* Portsmouth, NH: Heinemann.

Gilbert, C. (2014). A call for subterfuge: Shielding the ELA classroom from the restrictive sway of the Common Core. *The English Journal, 104*(2), 27–33.

Giouroukakis, V., & Honigsfeld, A. (2010). High-stakes testing and high school English learners: Using culturally and linguistically responsive literacy practices in the high school English classroom. *TESOL Journal, 1*(4), 470–499.

González, N., Moll, L. C., & Amanti, C. (2005). *Funds of knowledge: Theorizing practice in households, communities, and classrooms.* Mahwah, NJ: Lawrence Erlbaum Associates.

Goodwin, A. P., & Jiménez, R. (2015). TRANSLATE: New strategic approaches for English learners. *The Reading Teacher, 69*(6), 621–625.

Graves, D. H. (1983). *Writing: Teachers and children at work.* Exeter, NH: Heinemann Educational Books.

Guthrie, J. T., Wigfield, A., & You, W. (2012). Instructional contexts for engagement and achievement in reading. In S. Christenson, A. L. Reschly, & C. Wylie (Eds.), *Handbook of research on student engagement* (pp. 675–694). New York, NY: Springer.

Haag, C. C., & Compton, M. (2015). Tangled in Charlotte's Web: Lessons learned from English learners. In F. B. Boyd & C. H. Brock (Eds.), *Social diversity within multiliteracies: Complexity in teaching and learning* (pp. 127–143). New York, NY: Routledge.

Hall, E. T. (1976). *Beyond culture.* Garden City, NY: Anchor Press.

Harste, J. C. (2003). What do we mean by literacy now? *Voices from the Middle, 10*(3), 8–12.

Herrell, A. L., Jordan, M., & Herrell, A. L. (2012). *50 strategies for teaching English language learners* (4th ed.). Boston, MA: Pearson.

Honigsfeld, A., & Dove, M. G. (2013). *Common Core for the not-so-common learner: English language arts strategies grades 6–12.* Thousand Oaks, CA: Sage.

International Reading Association & National Council for Teachers of English. (2006). *Standards for the English language arts.* Available at http://www.ncte.org/library/NCTEFiles/Resources/Books/Sample/StandardsDoc.pdf

Ivey, G., & Broaddus, K. (2007). A formative experiment investigating literacy engagement among adolescent Latina/o students just beginning to read, write, and speak English. *Reading Research Quarterly, 42*(4), 512–545.

Ivey, G., & Johnston, P. H. (2013). Engagement with young adult literature: Outcomes and processes. *Reading Research Quarterly, 48*(3), 255–275.

Ivey, G., & Johnston, P. H. (2015). Engaged reading as a collaborative transformative practice. *Journal of Literacy Research, 47*(3), 297–327.

Jiménez, R. T., David, S., Fagan, K., Risko, V., Pacheco, M., Pray, L., & Gonzales, M. (2015). Using translation to drive conceptual development for students becoming literate in English as an additional language. *Research in the Teaching of English, 49*(3), 248–271.

King, A. (1993). From sage on a stage to guide on the side. *College Teaching, 41*(4), 30–35.

Klein, E., & Martohardjono, G. (2006). *Understanding the student with interrupted formal education (SIFE): A study of SIFE skills, needs and achievement.* New York, NY: New York City Department of Education.

Krashen, S. D. (1994). Bilingual education and second language acquisition theory. In C. F. Leyba (Ed.), *Schooling language minority students: A theoretical framework* (2nd ed., pp. 47–75). Los Angeles, CA: Evaluation, Dissemination and Assessment Center, School of Education, California State University, Los Angeles.

Krashen, S. D. (2004). *The power of reading: Insights from the research* (2nd ed.). Portsmouth, NH: Heinemann.

Krashen, S. D. (2012). Developing academic language. Some hypotheses. *Journal of Foreign Language Teaching, 7*(2), 8–15.

Ladson-Billings, G. (1995). Toward a theory of culturally relevant pedagogy. *American Educational Research Journal, 32*(3), 465–491.

Landay, E., Wootton, K., & Heath, S. B. (2012). *A reason to read: Linking literacy and the arts.* Cambridge, MA: Harvard Education Press.

Layne, S. L. (2015). *In defense of read-aloud: Sustaining best practice.* Portland, ME: Stenhouse Publishers.

Lewis, C., & Dockter, J. (2011). Reading literature in secondary school: Disciplinary discourses in global times. In S. A. Wolf, K. Coats, P. Enciso, & C. A. Jenkins (Eds.), *Handbook of research on children's and young adult literature* (pp. 76–91). New York, NY: Routledge.

Long, M. H. (1996). The role of the linguistic environment in second language acquisition. In W. Ritchie & T. Bhatia (Eds.), *Handbook of second language acquisition* (pp. 487–535). Malden, MA: Blackwell.

Luke, A. (2012). After the testing: Talking and reading and writing the world. *Journal of Adolescent & Adult Literacy, 56*(1), 8–13.

Martínez, R. A. (2010). Spanglish as literacy tool: Toward an understanding of the potential role of Spanish-English code-switching in the development of academic literacy. *Research in the Teaching of English, 45*(2), 124–149.

Martínez-Alba, G., & Cruzado-Guerrero, J. (2015). *Wordless books: So much to say!* Alexandria, VA: TESOL Press.

Martínez-Roldán, C. M., & Newcomer, S. (2011). "Reading between the pictures": Immigrant students' interpretations of The Arrival. *Language Arts, 88*(3), 188–197.

Mather, M. (2009). *Children in immigrant families chart new path.* Washington, DC: Population Reference Bureau.

Menken, K. (2008). *English learners left behind: Standardized testing as language policy.* Clevedon, England: Multilingual Matters.

Menken, K. (2013). Emergent bilingual students in secondary school: Along the academic language and literacy continuum. *Language Teacher, 46*(4), 438–476.

Menken, K., & Kleyn, T. (2010). The long-term impact of subtractive schooling in the educational experiences of secondary English language learners. *International Journal of Bilingual Education and Bilingualism, 13*(4), 399–417.

Mercado, C. I. (2005). See what's there: Language and literacy funds of knowledge in New York Puerto Rican homes. In A. C. Zentella (Ed.), *Building on strength:*

Language and literacy in Latino families and communities (pp. 134–147). New York, NY: Teachers College Press.

Migration Policy Institute. (2015). *Children under 18 in immigrant and native families.* Available at http://www.migrationpolicy.org/programs/data-hub/charts/children-immigrant-families

Moeller, R. (2016). A question of legitimacy: Graphic novel reading as "real" reading. *Journal of Adolescent & Adult Literacy, 59*(6), 709–717.

Murillo, L. A. (2016). Aquí no hay pobrecitos: Decolonizing bilingual teacher education in the U.S.-Mexico borderlands. *Diaspora, Indigenous, and Minority Education,* 1–14.

Newman, B. M. (2012). Mentor texts and funds of knowledge: Situating writing within our students' worlds. *Voices from the Middle, 20*(1), 25–30.

Nieto, S., & Bode, P. (2012). *Affirming diversity: The sociopolitical context of multicultural education* (6th ed.). Boston, MA: Pearson Education.

Olsen, L. (2010). *Reparable harm: Fulfilling the unkept promise of educational opportunity for California's long term English learners.* Long Beach, CA: Californians Together.

Olson, C. B., Scarcella, R. C., & Matuchniak, T. (2015). *Helping English learners to write: Meeting common core standards, grades 6–12.* New York, NY: Teachers College Press.

Optiz, M. F., & Rasinski, T. V. (1998). *Good-bye round robin: 25 effective oral reading strategies.* Portsmouth, NH: Heinemann.

Orellana, M. F. (2009). *Translating childhoods: Immigrant youth, language, and culture.* New Brunswick, NJ: Rutgers University Press.

Ortega, L. (2009). *Understanding second language acquisition.* New York, NY: Routledge.

Parris, H., Estrada, L., & Honigsfeld, A. (2017). *ELL Frontiers: Using technology to enhance instruction for English learners.* Thousand Oaks, CA: Sage.

Patterson, L., Holladay, R. J., & Eoyang, G. H. (2013). *Radical rules for schools: Adaptive action for complex change.* Circle Pines, MN: Human Systems Dynamics Institute.

Pérez Rosario, V. (2014). *The CUNY-NYSIEB guide to translanguaging in Latino/a literature.* Available at http://www.cuny-nysieb.org/wp-content/uploads/2016/05/CUNY-NYSIEB-Latino-Literature-Guide-Final-January-2015.pdf

Rader, W. (2017). *The online slang dictionary.* Retrieved from http://onlineslangdictionary.com/meaning-definition-of/keep-it-real

Rosenblatt, L. M. (1940). Moderns among masterpieces. *The English Leaflet, 39*(350), 98–110.

Rosenblatt, L. M. (1978). *The reader, the text, the poem: The transactional theory of the literary work.* Carbondale, IL: Southern Illinois University Press.

Rosenblatt, L. M. (2005). *Making meaning with texts: Selected essays.* Portsmouth, NH: Heinemann.

Ruiz, R. (1997). The empowerment of language minority students. In A. Darder, R. D. Torres, & H. Gutiérrez (Eds.), *Latinos and education: A critical reader* (pp. 319–328). New York, NY: Routledge.

Rumbaut, R. G. (2014). English plus: Exploring the socioeconomic benefits of bilingualism in Southern California. In R. M. Callahan & P. C. Gándara (Eds.), *The bilingual advantage: Language, literacy, and the labor market* (pp. 182–205). Bristol, England: Multilingual Matters.

Sadowski, M. (2013). *Portraits of promise: Voices of successful immigrant students.* Cambridge, MA: Harvard Education Press.

Salinas, C. (2006). Educating late arrival high school immigrant students: A call for a more democratic curriculum. *Multicultural Perspectives, 8*(1), 20–27.

Santibañez, L., & Zárate, M. E. (2014). Bilinguals in the U.S. and college enrollment. In R. M. Callahan & P. C. Gándara (Eds.), *The bilingual advantage: Language, literacy, and the labor market* (pp. 211–233). Bristol, England: Multilingual Matters.

Sciurba, K. (2014). Texts as mirrors, texts as windows: Black adolescent boys and the complexities of textual relevance. *Journal of Adolescent & Adult Literacy, 58*(4), 308–316.

Short, D. J., & Boyson, B. A. (2012). *Helping newcomer students succeed in secondary schools and beyond.* Washington, DC: Center for Applied Linguistics.

Sims, R. (1983). Strong black girls: A ten year old responds to fiction about Afro-Americans. *Journal of Research and Development in Education, 16*(3), 21–28.

Sims Bishop, R. (1990). Mirrors, windows, and sliding glass doors. *Perspectives: Choosing and using books for the classroom, 6*(3), ix–xi.

Skerrett, A. (2015). *Teaching transnational youth: Literacy and education in a changing world.* New York, NY: Teachers College Press.

Smetana, K., Odelson, D., Burns, H., & Grisham, D. (2009). Using graphic novels in the high school classroom: Engaging deaf students with a new genre. *Journal of Adolescent & Adult Literacy, 53*(3), 228–240.

Stewart, M. A. (2013). "What up" and "TQM": English learners writing on Facebook to acquire English and express their Latina/o identities. In K. E. Pytash & R. E. Ferdig (Eds.), *Exploring technology for writing and writing instruction* (pp. 328–344). Hershey, PA: IGI Global.

Stewart, M. A. (2014). Social networking, workplace, and entertainment literacies: The out-of-school literate lives of newcomer Latina/o adolescents. *Literacy Research and Instruction, 53*(4), 347–371.

Stewart, M. A. (2015). "My journey of home and peace": Learning from adolescent refugees' lived experiences. *Journal of Adolescent & Adult Literacy, 59*(2), 149–159.

Stewart, M. A. (2016). Nurturing care relationships through five simple rules. *English Journal, 105*(3), 22–28.

Stewart, M. A. (2017). *Understanding adolescent immigrants: Moving toward an extraordinary discourse for extraordinary youth.* Lanham, MD: Lexington Books.

Stewart, M. A., & Hansen-Thomas, H. (2016). Sanctioning a space for translanguaging in the secondary English class: A case of a transnational youth. *Research in the Teaching of English, 50*(4), 450–472.

Suárez-Orozco, C., Suárez-Orozco, M. M., & Todorova, I. (2008). *Learning a new land: Immigrant students in American society.* Cambridge, MA: Belknap Press of Harvard University Press.

Sutherland, L. M. (2005). Black adolescent girls' use of literacy practices to negotiate boundaries of ascribed identity. *Journal of Literacy Research, 37*(3), 365–406.

Swain, M. (1985). Communicative competence: Some roles of comprehensible input and comprehensible output in its development. In S. M. Gass & C. G. Madden (Eds.), *Input in second language acquisition* (pp. 235–253). Rowley, MA: Newberry House.

Thomas, W. P., & Collier, V. P. (2012). *Dual language education for a transformed world.* Albuquerque, NM: Dual Language Education of New Mexico.

Tse, L. (1996). Language brokering in linguistic minority communities: The case of Chinese- and Vietnamese-American students. *Bilingual Research Journal, 20*(3–4), 485–498.

Turney, K., & Kao, G. (2009). Barriers to school involvement: Are immigrant parents disadvantaged? *Journal of Educational Research, 102*(4), 257–271.

Tytel, M., & Holladay, R. (2011). *Simple rules: A radical inquiry into self.* Apache Junction, AZ: Gold Canyon Press.

U.S. Department of Education, Institute of Education Sciences, National Center for Education Statistics. (2016). Diversity in home languages: Examining English learners in U.S. public schools. Available at https://nces.ed.gov/blogs/nces/post/diversity-in-home-languages-examining-english-learners-in-u-s-public-schools

Valdés, G., Menken, K., & Castro, M. (2015). *Common core, bilingual and English language learners: A resource for educators.* Philadelphia, PA: Caslon Publishing.

Valenzuela, A. (1999). *Subtractive schooling: U.S.-Mexican youth and the politics of caring.* Albany, NY: State University of New York Press.

Van Lier, L. (2000). From input to affordance: Social-interactive learning from an ecological perspective. In P. Lantolf (Ed.), *Sociocultural theory and second language learning* (pp. 155–177). Oxford, England: Oxford University Press.

Wickstrom, C., Araujo, J., Patterson, L., Hoki, C., & Roberts, J. (2011). Teachers prepare students for career and college: "I see you," therefore I can teach you. In P. J. Dunston, L. B. Gambrell, K. Headly, S. K. Fullerton, P. M. Stecker, V. R. Gillis, & C. C. Bates (Eds.), *60th Yearbook of the Literacy Research Association* (pp. 113–126). Oak Creek, WI: Literacy Research Association.

WIDA. (2015). *SLIFE: Students with limited or interrupted formal education.* Board of Regents at the University of Wisconsin System. Available at https://www.wida.us/get.aspx?id=848

Wright, W. E. (2010). *Foundations for teaching English language learners: Research, theory, policy, and practice.* Philadelphia, PA: Caslon, Inc.

Yi, Y. (2007). Engaging literacy: A biliterate student's composing practices beyond school. *Journal of Second Language Writing, 13*(1), 23–39.

Yi, Y. (2010). Adolescent multilingual writers' transitions across in- and out-of-school writing contexts. *Journal of Second Language Writing, 19*(1), 17–32.

Literature Cited

Ada, A. F., & Zubizarreta, G. M. (2011). *Dancing home.* New York, NY: Atheneum Books for Young Readers.

Ada, A. F., & Campoy, F. I. (2013). *¡Sí! Somos Latinos.* Doral, FL: Santillana.

Adler, D. A., & Casilla, R. (1993). *A picture book of Rosa Parks.* New York, NY: Holiday House.

Alexander, K. (2014). *The crossover.* Boston, MA: Houghton Mifflin Harcourt.

Álvarez, J. (2006a). *En busca de milagros.* New York, NY: Alfred A. Knopf Books for Young Readers.

Álvarez, J. (2006b). *Finding miracles.* Carmel, CA: Hampton-Brown.

Álvarez, J. (2010). *Return to sender.* New York, NY: Yearling.

Atkin, S. B. (1993). Fitting in. In S. B. Atkin (Ed.), *Voices from the fields: Children of migrant farmworkers tell their stories* (pp. 36–43). Boston, MA: Little Brown and Company.

Atkins, L., & Yogi, S. (2017). *Fred Korematsu speaks up.* Berkeley, CA: Heyday.

Banyai, I. (1995). *Zoom.* New York, NY: Viking.

Bell, C., & Lasky, D. (2014). *El Deafo.* New York, NY: Amulet Books.

Bernardo, A. (1996). *Fitting in.* Houston, TX: Piñata Books.

Bernier-Grand, C. T., & Gonzalez, T. (2010). *Sonia Sotomayor: Supreme court justice.* New York, NY: Marshall Cavendish Children's.

Betancourt, I. (2011). *Even silence has an end: My six years of captivity in the Colombian jungle.* London, England: The Penguin Press.

Boyne, J. (2006). *The boy in the striped pajamas: A fable.* Oxford, England: David Fickling Books.

Brown, M., & Paschkis, J. (2011). *Pablo Neruda: Poet of the people.* New York, NY: Henry Holt and Co.

Brown, S. (2014). *Caminar.* Somerville, MA: Candlewick Press.

Bruchac, J. (2006). *Code talker: A novel about the Navajo marines of World War Two.* New York, NY: Puffin.

Bryan, A. (2016). *Freedom over me: Eleven slaves, their lives and dreams brought to life.* New York, NY: Atheneum Books for Young Readers.

Buitrago J., & Yockteng, R. (2015). *Two white rabbits.* Toronto, Canada: Groundwood Books/House of Anansi Press.

Burciaga, J. A. (2005). Bilingual love poem. In L. M. Carlson (Ed.), *Red hot salsa: Bilingual poems on being young and Latino in the United States* (p. 72). New York, NY: Holt.

Carlson, L. M. (2005). *Red hot salsa: Bilingual poems on being young and Latino in the United States.* New York, NY: Henry Holt.

Carlson, L. M. (2013). *Cool salsa: Bilingual poems on growing up Hispanic in the United States.* New York, NY: Square Fish.

Castilla, J. M. (1999). *Emilio.* Houston, TX: Piñata Books.

Castilla, J. M. (2009). *Strange parents.* Houston, TX: Piñata Books.

Cha, D., Cha, C., Cha, N. T., & Minnesota Humanities Commission. (2002). *Dia's story cloth.* (Bilingual ed.). St. Paul, MN: Minnesota Humanities Commission.

Chikwanine, M., & Humphreys, J. D. (2015). *Child soldier: When boys and girls are used in war.* Toronto, Canada: Citizen Can Press.

Chin-Lee, C., Halsey, M., & Addy, S. (2005). *Amelia to Zora: Twenty-six women who changed the world.* Watertown, MA: Charlesbridge.

Chin-Lee, C., Halsey, M., & Addy, S. (2006). *Akira to Zoltán: Twenty-six men who changed the world.* Watertown, MA: Charlesbridge.

Coerr, E., & Himler, R. (1999). *Sadako and the thousand paper cranes.* New York, NY: Puffin.

Coerr, E., & Uyehara, H. C. (1993). *Mieko and the fifth treasure.* New York, NY: Putnam.

Cofer, J. O. (2004). *Call me María: A novel.* New York, NY: Orchard Books.

Colato Laínez, R., & Graullera Ramírez, F. (2009). *René has two last names.* Houston, TX: Piñata Books.

Cole, H. (2012). *Unspoken: A story from the Underground Railroad.* New York, NY: Scholastic Press.

Conkling, W. (2011). *Sylvia and Aki.* Berkeley, CA: Tricycle Press.

Corcoran, J. (2012). *Dare to dream . . . change the world.* Tulsa, OK: Kane Miller Publishing.

Curtis, C. P. (1995). *The Watsons go to Birmingham—1963.* Austin, TX: Holt, Reinhart and Winston.

Danticat, E. (2002). *Behind the mountains.* New York, NY: Scholastic.

Danticat, E., & Staub, L. (2015). *Mama's nightingale: A story of immigration and separation.* New York, NY: Dial Books for Young Readers.

Davis, J. (2014). *Spare parts: Four undocumented teenagers, one ugly robot, and the battle for the American dream.* New York, NY: Farrar, Straus, and Giroux.

De la Cruz, M. (2005). *Fresh off the boat.* New York, NY: HarperCollins.

De la Cruz, M., & Venditti, R. (2013). *Blue bloods: The graphic novel.* New York, NY: Hyperion Paperbacks.

Diaz, A. (2016). *The only road.* New York, NY: Simon & Schuster Books for Young Readers.

DiPiazza, F. (2008). *Democratic Republic of Congo in pictures.* Minneapolis, MN: Twenty-First Century Books.

Engle, M. (2008). *The surrender tree: Poems of Cuba's struggle for freedom* (Bilingual ed.). New York, NY: Henry Holt and Co.

Engle, M. (2015). *Enchanted air: Two cultures, two wings: A memoir.* New York, NY: Atheneum Books for Young Readers.

Feelings, M. L., & Feelings, T. (1974). *Jambo means hello: Swahili alphabet book.* New York, NY: Dial Press.

Fitzmaurice, K. (2012). *A diamond in the desert.* New York, NY: Viking.

Fraillon, Z. (2016). *The bone sparrow.* New York, NY: Disney-Hyperion.

Galisky, A. F., & Shine, R. (2010). *Papers: Stories by undocumented youth.* Portland, OR: Graham Street Productions.

Gallo, D. R. (2004). *First crossing: Stories about teen immigrants.* Cambridge, MA: Candlewick Press.

Grande, R. (2012). *The distance between us: A memoir.* New York, NY: Atria Books.

Green, J. (2012). *The fault in our stars.* New York, NY: Dutton Books.

Harley, A., & Noyes, D. (2009). *African acrostics: A word in edgeways.* Somerville, MA: Candlewick Press.

Hayes, J. (2004). *Ghost fever.* El Paso, TX: Cinco Puntos Press.

Heller, R. (1992). *Many luscious lollipops: A book about adjectives.* New York, NY: Sandcastle Books.

Ho, M. (2003). *The stone goddess.* New York, NY: Orchard Books.

Ho, M. (2004). The green armchair. In D. R. Gallo (Ed.), *First crossing: Stories about teen immigrants* (pp. 201–224). Cambridge, MA: Candlewick Press.

Jiménez, F. (2000). *Cajas de cartón: Relatos de la vida peregrina de un niño campesino.* Boston, MA: Cengage Learning.

Jiménez, F. (2002). *Senderos fronterizos: Continuación de cajas de cartón.* Boston, MA: Houghton Mifflin.

Jiménez, F. (2009). *Más allá de mí: Continuación de cajas de cartón y senderos fronterizos.* Boston, MA: Houghton Mifflin.

Jiménez, J. (2016). *Bloodline.* Houston, TX: Piñata Books.

Joffo, J., & Bailly, V. (2013). *A bag of marbles.* Minneapolis, MN: Learner Publishing.

Johng-Nishikawa, J. (2011). *Dreaming in English: A memoir.* Davis, CA: Yellow Tree.

Judge, L. (2007). *One thousand tracings: Healing the wounds of World War II.* New York, NY: Hyperion Books for Children.

Kerley, B. (2002). *A cool drink of water.* Washington, DC: National Geographic Society.

Kramer, A. (2009). *World history biographies: Anne Frank: The young writer who told the world her story.* Washington, DC: National Geographic.

Khan, M. (2011). *The hijab boutique.* Leicestershire, England: The Islam Foundation.

King, D. (2014). *I see the sun in Myanmar (Burma).* Hardwick, MA: Satya House Publications.

Lai, T. (2011). *Inside out & back again.* New York, NY: Harper.

Lee-Tai, M. (2006). *A place where sun flowers grow.* New York, NY: Children's Book Press.

Leitner, I., & Pedersen, J. (1992). *The big lie: A true story.* New York, NY: Scholastic.

Levine, E., & Björkman, S. (1989). *I hate English!* New York, NY: Scholastic.

Lewis, J. P. (2012). The child. In J. Corcoran (Ed.), *Dare to dream* (p. 2). Tulsa, OK: Kane Miller Publishing.

Leyson, L. (2015). *The boy on the wooden box: How the impossible became possible . . . on Schindler's list.* New York, NY: Atheneum Books for Young Readers.

Lowry, L. (1989). *Number the stars.* Boston, MA: Houghton Mifflin.

Lyon, G. E. (1999). *Where I'm from: Where poems come from.* Spring, TX: Absey & Co.

Marston, E. (2008). *Santa Claus in Baghdad and other stories about teens in the Arab world.* Bloomington, IN: Indiana University Press.

McCall, G. G. (2012). *Summer of the mariposas.* New York, NY: Tu Books.

McCall, G. G. (2016). *Shame the stars.* New York, NY: Tu Books.

Medina, J., & Casilla, R. (2004). *The dream on Blanca's wall: Poems in English and Spanish.* Honesdale, PA: Wordsong/Boyds Mills Press.

Medina, J., & Vanden Broeck, F. (1999). *My name is Jorge on both sides of the river: Poems.* Honesdale, PA: Wordsong/Boyds Mills Press.

Miller, R. J. (2013). *A humble village.* Lexington, KY: Robin Joyce Miller.

Mobin-Uddin, A., & Kiwak, B. (2005). *My name is Bilal.* Honesdale, PA: Boyds Mills Press.

Mochizuki, K., & Lee, D. (1993). *Baseball saved us.* New York, NY: Lee & Low.

Mochizuki, K., & Lee, D. (1997). *Passage to freedom: The Sugihara story.* New York, NY: Lee & Low Books.

Moss, M. (2013). *Barbed wire baseball.* New York, NY: Abrams Books for Young Readers.

Myers, W. D. (1993). *Malcolm X: By any means necessary.* New York, NY: Scholastic.

Na, A. (2006). *Wait for me.* New York, NY: G. P. Putnam's Sons.

Na, A. (2016). *A step from heaven* (1st Atheneum paperback ed.). New York, NY: Simon & Schuster.

Nakazawa, K. (1987). *Pies descalzos 1: Una historia de Hiroshima.* New York, NY: Random House.

Namioka, L. (2003). The all-American slurp. In B. Preston (Ed.), *A sense of wonder* (pp. 19–29). White Plains, NY: Longman.

Nazario, S. (2013). *Enrique's journey: The true story of a boy determined to reunite with his mother.* New York, NY: Delacorte Press.

Nelson, M. (2005). *A wreath for Emmett Till.* Boston, MA: Houghton Mifflin.

Nye, N. S. (1995). *The tree is older than you are: A bilingual gathering of poems & stories from Mexico with paintings by Mexican artists.* New York, NY: Simon & Schuster Books for Young Readers.

Nye, N. S. (1997). *Habibi.* New York, NY: Simon & Schuster Books for Young Readers.

Nye, N. S. (2002). *19 varieties of gazelle: Poems of the Middle East.* New York, NY: Greenwillow Books.

Nye, N. S. (2014). *The turtle of Oman: A novel.* New York, NY: Greenwillow Books.

Palacio, R. J. (2013). *Wonder.* Waterville, ME: Thorndike Press.

Park, L. S. (2010). *A long walk to water: Based on a true story.* New York, NY: Houghton Mifflin Harcourt.

Parks, R., & Haskins, J. (1992). *Rosa Parks: My story.* New York, NY: Dial Books.

Parks, R., & Reed, G. J. (1996). *Dear Mrs. Parks: A dialogue with today's youth.* New York, NY: Lee & Low Books.

Paschen, E., & Raccah, D. (2010). *Poetry speaks who I am*. Naperville, IL: Sourcebooks/Jabberwocky.

Pinkney, A. D., & Pinkney, J. B. (2008). *Boycott blues: How Rosa Parks inspired a nation*. New York, NY: Greenwillow Books.

Preus, M., & Takahashi, H. (2008). *The peace bell*. New York, NY: Henry Holt.

Ramos, J. (2005). *Morir en el intento: La peor tragedia de inmigrantes en la historia de los Estados Unidos*. New York, NY: Harper Collins Publishers.

Ramos, J., & Cordero, K. (2005). *Dying to cross: The worst immigrant tragedy in American history*. New York, NY: Rayo.

Reynolds, A., & Cooper, F. (2009). *Back of the bus*. New York, NY: Philomel Books.

Rodger, E. (2017). *Leaving my homeland: A refugee's journey from the Democratic Republic of the Congo*. St. Catherine's, Ontario: Crabtree Publishing Company.

Rubin, S. G. (2011). *Irena Sendler and the children of the Warsaw Ghetto*. New York, NY: Holiday House.

Rubin, S. G. (2013). *Diego Rivera: An artist for the people*. New York, NY: Abrams Books for Young Readers.

Ruelle, K. G., & DeSaix, D. D. (2009). *The grand mosque of Paris: A story of how Muslims rescued Jews during the Holocaust*. New York, NY: Holiday House.

Rush, E. (2011). *M is for Myanmar*. San Francisco, CA: Things Asian Press.

Ruurs, M. (2016). *Stepping stones: A refugee family's journey*. Victoria, British Columbia, Canada: Orca Book Publishers.

Ryan, P. M. (2000). *Esperanza rising*. New York, NY: Scholastic Press.

Sack, J. (2015). *La Lucha: The story of Lucha Castra and human rights in Mexico*. Brooklyn, NY: Verso.

Sánchez, T. (1994). Why am I so brown? In L. M. Carlson (Ed.), *Cool salsa: Bilingual poems on growing up Latino in the United States*. (pp. 98–99). New York, NY: Holt.

Shea, P. D. (2003). *Tangled threads: A Hmong girl's story*. New York, NY: Clarion Books.

Smith, I. (2001). *The lonely queue: The forgotten history of the courageous Chinese Americans in Los Angeles*. Manhattan Beach, CA: East West Discovery Press.

Smith, I. (2008). *Mei Ling in China City*. Manhattan Beach, CA: East West Discovery Press.

Smith, I., & Kindert, J. C. (2013). *Three years and eight months*. Manhattan Beach, CA: East West Discovery Press.

Soto, G. (2006). *Novio boy: A play*. Orlando, FL: Harcourt.

Stamaty, A. M. (2005). *Muhimat Al Sayyda Alia: Inkaz Kuttub Al Iraq [Alia's Mission: Saving the Books of Iraq]*. New York, NY: Alfred A. Knopf.

St. John, W. (2012). *Outcasts united: The story of a refugee soccer team that changed a town*. New York, NY: Delacorte Press.

Takei, G. (2017). George Takei: Internment, America's great mistake. *New York Times*. Available at https://www.nytimes.com/2017/04/28/opinion/george-takei-japanese-internment-americas-great-mistake.html?_r=0

Tan, S. (2006). *The arrival*. South Melbourne, Australia: Lothian Books.

Tan, S. (2011). *Lost and found.* New York, NY: Arthur A. Levine Books, an imprint of Scholastic Inc.

Thimmesh, C., & Sweet, M. (2000). *Girls think of everything: Stories of ingenious inventions by women.* Boston, MA: Houghton Mifflin.

Thompson, L. A., & Qualls, S. (2015). *Emmanuel's dream: The true story of Emmanuel Ofosu Yeboah.* New York, NY: Schwartz & Wade Books.

Tonatiuh, D. (2013). *Pancho Rabbit and the coyote: A migrant's tale.* New York, NY: Abrams Books for Young Readers.

Tonatiuh, D. (2014). *Separate is never equal: Sylvia Mendez & her family's fight for desegregation.* New York, NY: Abrams Books for Young Readers.

Tonatiuh, D., & Rivera, D. (2011). *Diego Rivera: His world and ours.* New York, NY: Abrams Books for Young Readers.

Tran, G. B. (2010). *Vietnamerica: A family's journey.* New York, NY: Villard Books.

Tran, T., & Phong, A. (2003). *Going home, coming home.* San Francisco, CA: Children's Book Press.

Vardell, S. M., & Wong, J. (2015). *The poetry Friday anthology for celebrations: Holiday poems for the whole year in English and Spanish.* Princeton, NJ: Pomelo Books.

Venkatraman, P. (2014). *A time to dance.* New York, NY: Speak.

Wells, R., & Yoshi. (1992). *A to Zen: A book of Japanese culture.* New York, NY: Simon & Schuster.

Whelan, G. (2004). *Chu Ju's house.* New York, NY: HarperCollins Publishers.

White, E. B. (1952). *Charlotte's web.* New York, NY: Harper & Brothers.

Wiesner, D. (2006). *Flotsam.* New York, NY: Clarion Books.

Wilson, T. (2016). *Through my eyes.* Edina, MN: Beaver's Pond Press.

Winter, J. (2002). *Béisbol: Pioneros y leyendas del béisbol latino.* New York, NY: Lee & Low Books.

Winter, J. (2010). *Biblioburro: A true story from Colombia.* New York, NY: Beach Lane Books.

Winter, J., & Juan, A. (2002). *Frida.* New York, NY: Arthur A. Levine Books, an imprint of Scholastic Inc.

Winter, J., Rodriguez, E., & Palacios, A. (2009). *Sonia Sotomayor: A judge grows in the Bronx = La juez que creció en el Bronx.* New York, NY: Atheneum Books for Young Readers.

Yolen, J., & Shannon, D. (1992). *Encounter.* San Diego, CA: Harcourt Brace Jovanovich.

Yoon, N. (2016). *The sun is also a star.* New York, NY: Delacorte Press.

Index

Note: *Italicized* page numbers indicate a glossary definition.

About the Author

Mary Amanda (Mandy) Stewart is assistant professor in the Department of Reading at Texas Woman's University in Denton, Texas, and a member of the North Star of Texas Writing Project, a local affiliate of the National Writing Project. Her research focuses on the biliteracy and language development of middle and high school students who are learning English as a second language. She is the "biblioburra", the book donkey, who loves to bring new books to multilingual adolescents for them to read and share their responses with her. She currently is learning with high school students and teachers through the *ELLevate!* grant from the U.S. Department of Education, which she directs.

Her research with adolescents learning English has appeared in various journals, including *Journal of Adolescent & Adult Literacy, The English Journal, Research in the Teaching of English, Literacy Research & Instruction,* and *TESOL Journal.* She is also the author of *Understanding Adolescent Immigrants: Moving Toward an Extraordinary Discourse for Extraordinary Youth* published with Lexington Books. Find her on Twitter, @drmandystewart.